Praise For

NEVER RUN A DEAD KATA

"I can highly recommend Mr. (Brother) Boyd's book. He has earned an eighth degree black belt in Christianity. Mr. Boyd lives what he espouses. His common sense approach to all aspects of life is refreshing, entertaining and a road map to eternal life. I'm proud to be walking this life path with Rodney Boyd."

Joey Monteleone, Radio/T.V. Host, Master Fisherman
2nd Degree (Ni Dan) Black Belt

"An inspirational look into a life that is dedicated to God's will and purpose. An encouragement to the readers facing challenges of their own to know with faith their own mountains can be climbed."

Sarah Zapotocky
2nd Degree (Ni Dan) Black Belt

"*Never Run A Dead Kata* is a truly captivating and inspirational journey that encourages the reader to explore their own path to living and to get out of life what they put into it. On the surface and due to their historical association with mystical secrets, cults and religious practices, martial arts and Christianity are often misunderstood to be in direct contrast with one another. Through this clever concoction of personal experiences, Mr. Boyd blends the ingredients of Christianity, Music, Humor, Martial Arts and Film to break these contrasts and reveal many connections and similarities necessary for living a peaceful and fulfilling life. It is a perfect illustration that success is a journey, not a destination."

Brian H. Williams
1st Degree (Sho Dan) Black Belt

"*Never Run A Dead Kata* is a great read. Rodney easily blends humor, witticisms and great use of the Word of God to bring out life lessons learned through his own experiences. You will laugh, you will cry and you may even find yourself in some of Rodney's stories.

Alan Smith, Assistant Missions Pastor
Springhouse Worship & Arts Center

"I have had the privilege to train with Mr. Boyd and under his instruction for the past four years. It is difficult to know whether he is a philosopher, a minister or a stand-up comedienne. I believe it is all of the above. His wit and knowledge are apparent in his writing, and his application of martial arts to life's ups and downs will keep you entertained."

Leslie Shearon, Registered Nurse
1st Degree (Sho Dan) Black Belt

"This Christian karate journey is well written, heartfelt and a deep and meaningful reflection of life. It is an essential read for any Christian martial artist. How do you run your kata or life; with an eye on the goal, aware of your need to live the life you have been given, or meaningless and allowing chance to choose your course?"

Paul Gratton, CEO
U.K. Aero

"With his usual humble sense of humor, Rodney provides an endearing story of his martial arts journey. In sharing his life experiences and Christian perceptions, he provides inspiration to the mind, body and soul. The *Way of Harmony* resonates in the life of my dear friend Rodney Boyd."

Karen Wilson, MSN RN
4th Degree (Yon Dan) Black Belt

"Rodney paints a beautiful picture of what our Christian walk should look like filled with passion, accuracy and intensity. His knowledge of God's word mixed with his witty humor makes for a great read and one that is easily applied to our life in the Nitty Gritty."

Mike Priebe, Owner
Memorypeel

"In **Never Run A Dead Kata**, Rodney Boyd shares his experiences of life, hope and faith through the eyes of a student of Karate. His comparisons of scripture with the themes of Karate held my interest and taught me at the same time. His personal story will bring hope to anyone who must overcome obstacles to reach their goals in life."

Bruce Coble, Missions Pastor
Springhouse Worship & Arts Center

"Mr. Boyd has blended his training in the martial arts and his lifelong spiritual pursuits brilliantly. This book is a must read for anyone who might also be on that lifelong journey of a Martial Life as well as the more important art of living a peaceful existence. Mr. Boyd inspires, enhances and builds lives on a daily basis, he makes you proud to call him a friend."

Michael Wilson, Owner
Peril Defense Products
3rd Degree (San Dan) Black Belt

"**Never Run A Dead** Kata is more than just they name of a book. It is the philosophy Rodney transparently lives his life by. The first time I heard the phrase was in a white belt class Rodney was teaching. The words hold true weather you are attempting the journey to black belt or mastery of the katas of life as we strive to be more like the master teacher, Jesus Christ. Rodney shares his love of The Lord, family, friends and mastery of karate to inspire and entertain the reader as only he can. I count it a blessing to know him."

Michael Moore, Training Specialist
Morphotrust USA
Purple Belt on the journey to Black Belt

"I give the book an "E," for everyone. This book is about the art of living life to the fullest and making the most of every situation. Live life with passion, determination, character and Jesus and you will have discovered the root spirit to maximize the Kata or your life!"

Dr. Peter Camiolo
Revolution Chiropractic (Maximized Living)

"**Never Run A Dead Kata** is a must read for anyone interested in the martial arts and a must possession for any martial arts library. It is a delightful and refreshing look at the world of martial arts specifically and life in general!"

Sensei Ned Jackson Coleman, Attorney at Law
5th Degree (Go Dan) Black Belt

"Rodney Boyd's freshman book, **Never Run A Dead Kata**, is a fresh mix of his love of Ka-Ra-Ta; and his love and passion for Jesus Christ. Rodney presents a unique style of storytelling that helps draw the reader into the lessons that are taught in Wado Ryu Karate and in the Scriptures. Reading this book helped me understand and visualize different lessons and practices of Wado Ryu Karate; and the foundation one must build to be effective in this art. It also revealed how crucial the truths we find in the Bible are to our everyday lives.Rodney is a Grand Master at being able to teach you the basics of Wado Ryu by drawing from his own life experiences and from the Scriptures. This book is a must have for any Karate student or fan. *Look out man! That's called Ka-Ra-Ta.*"

David Mason
Student of Isshin-Ryu Karate

"As a fellow karateka in the Wado Ryu style and pursuing my Sho Dan rank, Mr. Boyd's book has stopped me, made me think, and has reminded me that the lessons we are learning in the dojo have great relevance to our daily lives and especially those who follow the Lord and Savior Jesus Christ. His learning and ability to express these lessons in his book are great reminders to not only those involved in any form of Martial Arts but for anyone who seeks to live a life that honors God, is in harmony with his or her fellow man, and is at peace with himself."

Jason Anderson
Brown Belt

NEVER RUN A DEAD KATA

Steve... my brother,
MAy PsAlm 37:4 be
yours All the days of
your Life.
                  much Love
                  &Rei-spect
                  Rodney 2014

Lessons I Learned in the Dojo

RODNEY BOYD

WordCrafts

Never Run A Dead Kata
    Lessons I Learned in the Dojo
Copyright © 2014
Rodney Boyd Ni Dan

Cover photography & design by David Warren

Published by WordCrafts Press
Tullahoma, TN 37388
www.wordcrafts.net

DEDICATION

This book is dedicated to Brenda Sue Boyd, my wife of 40 years, my friend, my companion and the love of my life. She has been with me every step of the journey as I learned these lessons. When I was in my late 40s I told her that I was going to start taking karate again when I turned 50 years old. She did not laugh or make fun of me, but encouraged me to go after my dreams. It is also dedicated to my son Phillip Stephen Boyd who has always inspired me to be a better man and father. I love you both.

Contents

ACKNOWLEDGEMENTS
(Thanx And A Tip O' Da Hat To One And All)

On my karate journey, there have been many people who have planted something different and valuable in me. I realize I will probably leave someone out, but here are just a few of the main players in my life.

To Master Hirinori Otsuka for developing Wado Ryu Karate.

To Sensei Newton Harris, who owned and operated Bushido School of Karate and was my first instructor back in 1973. He took a raw piece of clay and began the molding process. When I tested for my black belt, he came. The man who was with me at the beginning was there for me as I tested for the prize.

To Sensei Bill Herzer who was the next owner of the Bushido School of Karate. He helped me continue on my journey. Then and now he always encourages me to relax.

To Sensei Bill Taylor, the current owner of Bill Taylor's School of Karate. I met Mr. Taylor back in 1973 when he started karate, and linked back up when I turned 50. He has been and remains a source of encouragement. He pushes me beyond my doubts and stimulates me to keep on keeping on. When I tried the excuse that I was too old to start back taking karate, he told me of a lady who was 72 years old and got her black belt. Then he said, "What's your excuse." When I was on the verge of taking my black belt exam, I momentarily lost the fire. Mr. Taylor relit the passion with one of his patented pep talks.

To Senpai Mike Wilson, who more than once spoke words of encouragement to me when I was on the brink of giving up. It is an honor to count him as a mentor, an example and a friend.

To Sensei Ned Coleman, who instills within me the spirit of Wado. He prepared me for my black belt exam over and over with every class.

To Sensei Lane Wommack, who always pushes me physically and never fails to provide great insight in to the 'why' of the movements.

To Sensei John Patterson, who assumed leadership of the United States Eastern Wado Ryu Karate Federation, when his father Sensei Cecil T. Patterson passed away.

To my many instructors over the years, Mr. Joe Maxwell, Ms. Karen Wilson, Mr. Dean Cordell, Mr. Steve Holt and Mr. Mike Arnold, and to my fellow karatekas who moved up and down the floor with me. Thanx, and a Tip O' Da Hat to one and all.

FORWARD
With The Foreword

"Never run a dead kata."

- Master Hirinori Otsuka

The statement, "never run a dead kata," was made by the man who developed the style of karate that I practice - *Wado Ryu*. Wado Ryu is the study of "the way of peace/harmony." It breaks down like this, Wa (peace/harmony) Do (way) Ryu (style).

My quest for my black belt was a long and convoluted path. The *dojo* is considered to be the school as a whole, but it is more than the school. It is the workout area where you bow, step on the mats and begin the process of learning not only the physical aspects of karate - but the code of karate or the heartbeat of karate. Before we get into the lessons I learned in the dojo, I believe that it would be a good idea to let you know how I arrived at October 29, 2007, the day I earned my 1st Degree Black Belt.

Part of the process involved writing a paper entitled "What Earning a Black Belt Means to Me." I'm sharing it here to give you an overview of my journey.

What Earning A Black Belt Means To Me

- Rodney Boyd Ik Kyu

To understand what earning a black belt means to me, you must understand the beginning of my journey. The roots of my desire to earn a black belt extends back to the mid 1960s. My first exposure to the martial arts was through a movie (actually a series of eight movies) starring Peter Lorre as a character named Mr. Moto. Mr. Moto was a Charlie Chan-type detective. He was small, unimposing, wearing wire-rimmed glasses and a white suit. The difference between him and Charlie Chan was that he would not only use his detective smarts to solve a crime, but he would use ju jitsu against the bad guys. I was amazed at how this little; unimposing man was able to beat the bad guys, without shooting them, but by merely throwing them around. The size ratio did not compute, but the seeds of martial arts were planted deep in me.

My first physical encounter using martial arts was in the 6th grade (around 1963), and was based on what I saw in the Mr. Moto movies. I was not trained in the martial arts and I was definitely not physically up to the task. I was a scrawny, skinny, proverbial 98-pound weakling. I was standing in a hallway outside of the gymnasium at Mitchell-Neilson Elementary School when a larger student started picking on me. He was kidding around and I did not feel threatened at the time, but all of a sudden, I found myself grabbing this large, imposing person by his arm. I twisted my hips and threw him over my shoulder, or more likely my hips.

Everyone was surprised at what happened - including the people around me and the guy I threw over my shoulder - but nobody was more surprised than me. I had merely imitated what I saw in a movie on late night television. From that moment on I was fascinated with the martial arts. From 1963 to 1972, I would read karate books by Bruce Tegner and watch Elvis give somebody a karate chop in the movies. I even played around with my friends, as we flipped each other around in my backyard. But for some reason, I never cultivated that desire until 1972, when a fateful event rekindled my desire for a black belt.

1972 was an eventful year for me. I got married (and am still married to the same woman after 40 years), had a steady job and I got beat up on the side of the road in front of God, all my co-workers and the rest of the world passing by that day.

Another event in 1972 was an advertisement in the Daily News Journal for a karate class that was forming in Murfreesboro, Tennessee. The ad was little larger than a postage stamp, but it caught my eye. The cost of the class was $15 a month and was being taught by a man I knew, Mr. Newton Harris. After my encounter with my Goliath, I figured I needed to learn how to defend myself.

Our first class met in the basement of Crichlow Elementary School, and later moved to a dojo on Vine Street. The school was the Bushido School of Karate; the style was Wado Ryu.

At that time the climate for karate was hot. On television, Batman and Robin were kicking and punching the bad guys (Burt Ward, the actor who played Robin had a black belt in real life). In the movie "Billy Jack," Billy was taking his left foot and placing it on the right side of Mr. Posner's face, while telling Posner that there "was not a damn thing that he could do about it." On the radio, Carl Douglas was singing that "everybody was Kung Fu fighting, their fists were fast as lightning." "Kung Fu" was a hit T.V. show and Bruce Lee was making a name for himself as Kato on "The Green Hornet" and the TV show "Longstreet" (teaching blind lawyer James Franciscus martial arts). The "chop suey" movies were all the rage.

I signed up for karate along with a few friends and we had a ball. We practiced kata together, stretched every chance we got, and worked out at the dojo four times a week. The classes went on for two to three hours. It was hot, sweaty, tiring and fun!

I was young, semi-flexible and eager to learn. I would not be a punching bag for some redneck on the side of the road again. At that time my motivation for wanting to be a Black Belt was self-preservation and fear. I climbed up through the ranks to the point of being ready to test for my green belt, but through a series of circumstances, I dropped out. Money, time, desire - all fizzled out.

For the next few decades, my desire to get my black belt would ebb and flow. I'd watch karate movies, going over in my mind the things that I had learned, but I never could get back into it. Mr. Harris eventually sold the school to Mr. Bill Herzer. It would be 30 years before I set foot into a dojo again.

I told my wife Brenda and my son Phillip that when I turned 50, I would return to karate. My goal was to have my black belt by the time I was 55 years old. I made that declaration while I was in my 40s. I am currently in my 60s and still kicking.

When I was 48 years old, I took Phillip to a Wado Tournament in Columbia, Tennessee, and told him that I would someday be down there on the gym floor competing. Three years later, I was.

In September, 2001, I ran into Mr. Bill Taylor at Quiznos restaurant. Mr. Taylor now owned Bill Taylor's Bushido School of Karate. Brenda was with me as I introduced myself to him and told him that I was thinking about starting karate again. I told him my story, but confessed I thought I might be too old to start back again.

"A 70 year-old woman at the school just earned her black belt," he told me. "What's your excuse?"

That lady was Ms. Betty Coleman, who continues to be an inspiration to me to this day. I had no excuse, so I signed up for classes. I receive my white belt on November 15, 2001 and my Ik Kyu (Brown Belt) on November 17, 2006. On September 12, 2007, seven years from my first class, I received notification of my scheduled black belt exam.

What does earning a black belt mean to me? At this point - everything. Attaining a black belt is a personal challenge to finish what I started in 1972. It transcends my original intent of self-preservation. I am no longer motivated by the fear of getting beat up on the side of the road again. As I learned various techniques over the past seven years, the spirit and attitude of Wado Ryu have been instilled within me. The principles of the way of harmony and peace are now my goals, rather than the belt around the waist.

Now don't get me wrong, the belt around the waist will be wonderful. But the black belt virtues found in the student guide transcend the belt. Modesty, courtesy, integrity, self-control, perseverance and an indomitable spirit - traits that have been walked out by all of my instructors over the years - are now goals that I strive for in my quest for the black belt.

What does earning a black belt mean to me? It means accomplishing a goal that I will carry with me for the rest of my life; one that I will walk out before others coming up the ranks with their own vision and dreams of a black belt.

This road has not been an easy one. At times my body has weakened with various pulls, strains, aches and pains. At times the desire for a black belt was overwhelmed with the desire to lay down and quit. At times my confidence was lower than the mat my feet were standing on, but thanks to the encouragement, rebuke and understanding from my instructors and my fellow karatekas, I stand ready to enter the next level, where now I am ready to learn.

My real purpose and power come from my faith and love for God (Father, Son, Holy Ghost). Eric Liddle, a runner in the 1924 Olympics in Paris and later a missionary to China, whose story is chronicled in the movie "Chariots of Fire," is a source of inspiration for me. He stated, "I believe God made me for a purpose, but he also made me fast. And when I run, I feel His pleasure."

I am not fast, but I do feel His pleasure when I work out and compete. Liddle also gave the secret of his success, and I hope it will also be the secret to my success.

"The secret of my success over the 400 meters is that I ran the first 200 as hard as I could and then the second 200, with God's help, I ran it harder."

Thank you for this opportunity.

Rodney Boyd Ik Kyu

CHAPTER ICHI (ONE)
WANTED DEAD OR ALIVE

Before you can understand the difference between a dead or an alive kata, it would be good to define the word kata. In some styles this is called *forms*. Kata has been defined as a lot of things, including but not limited to:

(1) a dance
(2) pre-arranged moves
(3) practice for a real fight.

While there may be some of all of these aspects in a kata, but in its simplest definition a kata is a series of blocks, kicks, punches, movement, turns, techniques and transitions placed in an orderly arrangement for the purpose of practice. They vary in length, direction and technique, but the one thing they all have in common is they all begin and end with respect. We will say more about this thing called respect in the chapter entitled REI-SPECT.

After learning some basic moves, including blocks, punches and turns, you are ready to run the First Basic Kata. I learned this kata way back in 1973, when Bushido School of Karate was on Vine Street in Murfreesboro Tennessee. At that time it was operated by Sensei Newton Harris. When I started taking karate again in 2001, the first kata I ran was First Basic Kata. It had not changed one iota from 1973 to 2001 and has still not changed.

There are 20 moves in First Basic Kata, and in a later kata called Kushan Ku, there are 120 moves. When you first start learning a kata it is awkward, cumbersome and you have difficulty with its directional aspect - at least it was for me. I like to think that I am developing the skeleton of the kata or just getting the technical aspects down, the directional aspects. Do I turn left or right? Is it a high block or a low block? Do I move forward or backwards? The moves appear Frankensteinish because of the stilted plodding through the movements, but at some point when you no longer have to think of the moves, you begin to flow. You are in transition from dead kata to an alive kata. This is where you begin to make *the* kata, *your* kata. You begin to own the kata and flow in it.

Of course in a street attack you would not run a kata to defend yourself. As Sensei Bill Taylor states, "Fighting is a game of adjustments."

While the kata is a practice tool, it is not *only* a practice tool for technique; it is a practice tool for spirit and attitude. We should practice kata with spirit. As Sensei Ned Coleman instilled in us, "How we punch or kick or run kata in class, is how we would perform on the street." He instructs us to throw a kick as if we were in a fight. Throw it hard, throw it strategically and hit the target that you are aiming for. If you are punching for the nose, don't hit the shoulder.

Never run a dead kata means to run it with spirit and passion, and not just go through the motion. It does not mean to run it as fast as you can, blurring all of the moves, but to run it with passion and accuracy. We should approach everything we do with the same intensity as when we run a kata. As you approach life itself, run your life *alive*, not dead. Live your life with passion. Never live a dead life.

Senpai Steve Morris responded to a note that I placed on Facebook about *dead* versus *alive* kata. It was so good that I asked his permission to add his comment here.

"I liked your note about dead kata. I thought I would throw out a thought to you that you may or may not have heard before. Part of what distinguishes a live kata (kata) from a dead kata (igata) is your physical and mental openness. After the first low block in First Basic Kata, we follow it with a junzuki (moving forward front punch). A dead kata (igata) blindly follows this pattern like an automaton; the practitioner is mentally locked into this sequence. However, if my kata is alive (kata), I am mentally and physically open to the possibility of following that low block with any other technique. Every time one runs the kata, one must be prepared to do whatever is appropriate. I could follow that low block with a skip in side kick (yoko geri). I could follow it with a nagashi zuki, moving backward. I might choose to follow it with a junsuki (moving forward front punch), but that is a choice that I make each time. I'm just as mentally and physically prepared to do anything else. Clearly, we strive to make that choice be a reflexive choice, just like choosing to remove your hand from a hot stove, so that when we see an opening we strike automatically with the appropriate technique."

Senpai Steve Morris Sandan - Third Degree Black Belt

While this is not a technical manual on Wado Ryu karate, Mr. Morris brings out a great point - a dead kata is just running it without thought, but an alive kata will be cognizant to change as needed. A dead kata is like assembly line production - one thing after another, never changing. A live kata is like the beauty of a potter who does not mass produce a piece of art (ignata). Each piece, while having similarities, is individualized and different (kata).

So it is with a kata that is alive. The 20 moves in First Basic are the same, but it becomes alive when you make it your own. So it is with life. Everybody is living, but if you are just running the Rat Race as fast as you can, the best you can hope for is to end up being the #1 Rat. If instead you live life with passion and spirit and you will have an *alive* life, a kata life versus an ignata life.

Jesus told us of a life that is *alive*:

"The thief comes only in order that he may steal and may kill and may destroy. I came that they may have and enjoy life, and have it in abundance - to the full, till it overflows."

John 10:10 (*AB*)

When Jesus was being quizzed on what the most important command was to follow, he quoted from Deuteronomy 6:4-5.

"Jesus answered, the foremost is, Hear, O Israel; the Lord our God is one Lord; and you shall love the Lord your God with all your heart, and with all your soul, and with all you mind, and with all your strength. The second is this, You shall love your neighbor as yourself. There is no other commandment greater than these."

Mark 12:29-31

"Whatever you do, do your work heartily (from the soul) as for the Lord, rather than for men, knowing that from the Lord you will receive the reward of the inheritance. It is the Lord whom you serve."

Colossians 3:22-24 (*AB*)

I have found that if I live my life with a passion for the Lord in the good times, it affects how I am able to handle life in the bad times. How we think affects how we live. It is all about mindset, whether when we are running kata or we are living our life.

Napoleon Hill, author of the book "Think and Grow Rich," stated that "Whatever the mind can conceive, the mind can believe, and the mind can achieve." Jesus (who came way before Napoleon Hill) stated, *"Whatever you desire, when you pray believe that you receive them and you shall have them."* (Mark 11:24)

Again, Jesus states, *"All things are possible to him that believes."* (Mark 9:23) The Apostle Paul underscores this when he wrote, *"I can do all things through Christ who strengthens me."* (Philippians 4:13)

To run a kata that is alive your focus must be on what you *can do*, and not what you *can't do*. Approach kata with passion.

Never run a dead kata.

CHAPTER NI (TWO)
REI-SPECT
The Art of Bowing

Otis Redding wrote and recorded a song by the title of *Respect*. Later, Aretha Franklin recorded *Respect* and made it her anthem. Both were crying out for "just a little respect - just a little bit." At one point they spell it out. "R-E-S-P-E-C-T, Find out what it means to me. R-E-S-P-E-C-T. Take care, TCB." The Staple Singers sang their signature song *Respect Yourself*. "If you disrespect anybody that you run in to how in the world do you think anybody's s'posed to respect you." The chorus of the song then proclaims - "Respect yourself, respect yourself. If you don't respect yourself ain't nobody gonna give a good cahoot, na na na na. Respect yourself, respect yourself."

Well, I don't know about you, but I want somebody to give a "Good Cahoot" about me. There is nothing worse than a "Bad Cahoot," also know as, "No Respect." Rodney Dangerfield, the comedian, made a career with the punch line while tugging on his tie, "I don't get no respect."

> "Karate begins and ends with respect."
>
> -Gichin Funakoshi

I said all of this about respect because that's the Number One karate move that I learned within the dojo. Without the REI (bowing to show respect), all of the katas, punches, kicks, techniques, etc., are null and void. Everything begins and ends with respect. The word, "Rei," simply means "to bow," but those three small letters mean so much more. It is the meaning behind the bow. Many ask, and many are concerned about, the reason behind the bow. Some think that by bowing we are worshipping someone or something; that it is a mystical act which may violate our principles as Christians. We are taught in Sunday school that we are not to bow to any idols.

"Therefore also God highly exalted Him (Jesus), and bestowed on Him (Jesus), the name which is above every name, that at the name of Jesus every knee should bow, of those who are in heaven, and on earth, and under the earth, and that every tongue should confess that Jesus Christ is Lord, to the glory of God the Father."

Philippians 2:9-11

But this act of the bowing (rei) is not the worship of anyone or anything. It is merely an act of respect - or as I like to call it, REI-spect. At the dojo, to paraphrase a Jerry Lee Lewis song, there is "a whole lot of bowing goin' on." When we enter onto the dojo floor, we bow. Whenever a Black Belt comes on the floor, we bow. Whenever we start a class, we do a series of three bows. Whenever we begin techniques or kata, we bow. Whenever our instructor uses us as an example to teach something, we bow when he is finished. Whenever we kumite (freestyle sparring), we bow. Whenever we end the class, we bow. Whenever we go off of the dojo floor, we bow. Even if a dog comes into the dojo, they Bow Wow!

It's like doing standing sit-ups.

We bow on the command of, "Rei." I like to say that we are showing REI-spect. REI-spect is the most important move that I learned on the dojo floor. Without REI-spect all you have are moves and techniques. Before you can REI-spect anyone else you must first REI-spect yourself. That is what they teach you in class - self-REI-spect. It is like Jesus said when asked about the most important command. Out of hundreds of commands, He gave two.

"Jesus answered, The foremost is, Hear, O Lord; the Lord our God is one Lord; and you shall love the Lord your God with all your heart, and with all your soul, and with all your mind, and with all your strength. The second is this, you shall love your neighbor as yourself. There is no other commandment greater than these."

Mark 12:29-31

If you can't REI-spect yourself, you will never be able to REI-spect anyone - not your neighbor or your karate partner.

The proper bow is following these basic steps:

(1) heels together
(2) hands hanging down to the side
(3) bend at the waist
(4) as you bend at the waist, keep your eyes up and looking forward
(5) return to upright position.

That is the technical aspects of the bow, but the true bow is when we bow from within. It is like a kata. We start out just learning the kata, but at some point we internalize it and it becomes second nature as we run it. So it is with the internalized bow, to show respect.

Whenever we Rei, we are showing respect and expressing thanks to the object bowed towards. This is a principle that I have internalized as I have walked my journey as a Christian.

"Thank [God] in everything - no matter what the circumstances may be, be thankful and give thanks; for this is the will of God for you [who are] in Christ Jesus [The Revealer and Mediator of that will]."

I Thessalonians 5:18 (AB)

Being thankful, being respectful, respecting yourself and others becomes second nature when you do these things with purpose and intent.

We now know that we should *never run a dead kata*, and the same principle applies with the REI-spect. Never bow a dead bow. Sometimes I see children, and some teens and adults, bowing as quickly as the can when they are leaving the dojo floor. It is like blurring a move in a kata or multiple techniques where we mistakenly substitute speed over form.

Bow slowly and with purpose. Take the time to clear your mind, focus on the task ahead, as you enter into a state of being thankful that you are able to accomplish the task ahead of you. This

When we start and end class we bow three times:
(1) **Shomen Rei:** To the front including the flags of the United States (our country where we are free to practice our art) and the flag of Japan where Wado Ryu was developed, and to a picture of Master Hironori Otsuka, the man who developed the style of Wado Ryu. These bows are showing respect, much like a salute respecting and honoring these things.
(2) **Sensei/Senpai Rei:** We bow to our instructors. By bowing we are expressing thanks and respect for teaching us.
(3) **Otagani Rei:** We are bowing to each other and thanking each other for working with us.

principle applies on the dojo floor, but also to your nitty-gritty, everyday, mundane, daily life. When I do an internal bow, I personally do bow before my God, showing respect, clearing my mind, focusing on the task ahead of me, respecting those around me - even those who don't necessarily deserve my respect. Even when I am bowing in class, especially in the opening and closing bow, I always visualize bowing to my God, showing Him respect and being very thankful to Him.

I would like to end this chapter with my heels together, my hands hanging to the side of my body, my eyes ahead, clearing my mind of the worries and the cares of the world and waiting for the three letter command as I think of you reading this book.

Otagani Rei. Much REI-spect my friends.

CHAPTER SAN (THREE)
THE BASICS

I n the beginning, way back in 1973, when I first set foot in the dojo - first in the basement of Crichlow Elementary School and later on Vine Street - there was a sense that I was going to enter into my pre-conceived idea of what karate was all about based on my movie and television experience. To my surprise and disappointment we began with the basics. Of course, if I had thought about it, where else would we start but the basics?

In the Student Guide, the Belt Curriculum is laid out in a systematic, methodical fashion. We start out with the White Belt Curriculum and go all the way through to the Brown Belt Curriculum (with three degrees of brown including San Kyu, Ni Kyu and Ik Kyu). The next stage for your black belt is an examination on all you have learned through the entire curriculum. Before you get to the black belt examination, you must start at square one - the basics.

The very first section in the curriculum is the White Belt Curriculum. This is where you learn things like how and why you bow, a horse stance (kiba dachi), a front punch, a front kick and a high block. You then progress through the curriculum attaining belt after belt. I have the honor and opportunity to teach a couple of white belt classes. The ages range from young kids to older adults and everything in between. From the first time I stepped into a class as a white belt way back in 1972, to the present as I teach the white belts, I am still learning the basics.

In reality, at every level of the belt curriculum, we are learning the basics, especially for that certain belt level. In Wado Ryu Karate, as sanctioned by the Otsuka family in Japan, the level of the belt curriculum is:

(1) White Belt
(2) Gold Belt
(3) Orange Belt
(4) Blue Belt
(5) Purple Belt
(6) Green Belt
(7) Brown Belt (three degrees of brown)
(8) Black Belt (multiple degrees)

Throughout the journey, to mark our progress on each belt, we were rewarded tips. Tips were pieces of colored electrical tape wrapped on our belt. It is amazing how excited both kids, and adults got over a piece of electrical tape, but it showed that we were grasping the basics.

Back in the day - that would be 1972/73 - Sensei Harris took us on a field trip to Madison Tennessee so that we could watch a class made up of nothing but Black Belts. I remember being so excited to be in a room where I would be able to see the *stuff*. The *stuff* was all the *stuff* that I had seen in the movies, where the kicks and punches would somehow be slowed down as if in suspended animation, and the speed of the kicks and punches would crack in the air like two boards being slapped together. I think I may have actually been slightly salivating in anticipation.

Row after row of Black Belts lined up and began class exactly like we did in Murfreesboro, with the series of bows as the command Rei (bow) was made. The command of Yoi (open) went out and then right foot back, Hajimai (do it quickly). Then this group of super trained warriors stepped out with Jun Zuki (moving forward front punch).

What!?

They were going through the same things that I had learned as a white and yellow/gold belt - the basics!

As it turns out, to be able to do an effective Yoko Tobi Geri (flying side kick), you must become strong in the basic Mai Geri (front kick). You never get away from the basics. Sensei Bill Taylor tells us that he is still learning things from the First Basic Kata, and he has been practicing his art for more than 40 years. I have been to various seminars with the grandson of Master Otsuka, and each time he comes, the anticipation of the higher ways of karate rises. Yet he (and other masters) always teach the basics, and they bring out things that you would never think about.

The challenge when teaching the basics is to make it continually interesting and challenging. Sometimes I can see a question in my students' eyes. It's the same look that I had in my eye.

"When are we going to learn the flying triple summersault sidekick?"

The same is true in this life that we live. We learn the basics of the ABC's, but we never get away from them. Every time we write or read or speak, we put those basic letters that we learned early on into words. When we learned one plus one is two, we never abandon that fact, but build upon it.

In my walk as a Christian, I started out learning the basics, the elementary principals of the faith as I transitioned from a baby Christian to a mature Christian.

"For though by this time you ought to be teachers, you have need again for some one to teach you the elementary principles of the oracles of God, and you have come to need milk and not solid food. For every one who partakes only of milk is not accustomed to the word of righteousness, for he is a babe. But solid food is for the mature, who because of practice, have their senses trained to discern good and evil."

Hebrews 5:12-14

The thought is comparison of a baby and an adult. If an adult walks around acting like a baby, something is wrong. There is a maturity process. The baby starts off with milk and the mature adult eats solid

> Once you earn your black belt and the presentation where you take off your brown belt and the Sensei ties on the prize of your belt, you are told:
>
> *"Now, you are ready to learn."*

foods (meat). Then the writer of Hebrews speaks of leaving the elementary, or words of beginning, and pressing on to maturity.

"Therefore leaving the elementary (basics) teaching about the Christ, let us press on to maturity, not laying again a foundation of (1) repentance from dead works (2) faith towards God (3) of instruction about baptisms (plural) (4) laying on of hands (5) the resurrection of the dead (6) eternal judgment."

Hebrews 6:1-2

This does not mean that we just forget the elementary basic principles, but we do build on them. You never get away from the basics. Just as you progressed from a baby to an adult in the natural, learning the basics and building on them, and just as you start your spiritual journey as a baby Christian and hopefully progress into a mature Christian, so it is with the basics in the lessons I learned and continue to learn in Wado Ryu Karate. My basic stances will be foundational in all future stances.

In the Hebrews passage it speaks of practice and training and pressing on. In the dojo we learn the principles of the basics, but we must practice at home. We then come back to the dojo to be trained. We hone and fine tune what we learned, then practice and continue training for a lifetime.

CHAPTER SHI (FOUR)
FOUNDATIONS
Building A Strong House

In my past life - before I became a Speech-Language Pathologist - I held many odd jobs, trying to find my niche in life. At one point I became involved in construction. That really is humorous, because I am not very handy when it comes to building things. I cut wood, drove nails and went for whatever the boss-man wanted to get the job done. In my minds eye, I could not see what needed to be done, or what angles were needed to build a particular structure. But one thing I did learn: if you want to build a good house, you must have a good foundation. The foundation starts at the bottom, and affects everything all the way to the top.

So it is with karate. If you bypass a solid foundation, everything else that you do will be off kilter. There is a picture of a pyramid on the wall at Bill Taylor's Bushido School of Karate, demonstrating the progression of what is needed to build a solid karate edifice. This is an extension, a continuation, of the previous chapter on The Basics. The base (basic) of the pyramid model is The Foundation. The next level in the mid-range is Posture. The pinnacle of the pyramid is Technique.

If you focus only on technique without proper posture and poor foundation, your technique will be sloppy. You will be off-balance and ineffective. If you have a good foundation, but very poor posture, you may throw a technique but the technique will not effectively and strategically reach the target. But when foundation, posture and technique are in proper order, there is a synergistic quality of how you perform that applies not only on the dojo floor, but also in the street and in every area of your life.

FOUNDATION

Everything that we do on the dojo floor is based on foundation, and the foundation that we start with is proper stances. Stances are how you stand. All stances will be carried with you from white belt to black belt. From the moment you step on the dojo floor and until you walk off the dojo floor, everything will be based on stances.

MUSUBI DACHI (Attention Stance)

One of the foundational stances, and to me one of the most important stances, is Musubi Dachi. Musubi Dachi is the attention stance. The heels are placed together, toes at a 45 degree angle with the hands in front of you hanging down, eyes straight ahead. Why is this stance the most important one that we learn? It is the stance we use when we bow and enter onto the floor, and when we leave the floor at the end of class. It is the stance that we begin class with as we show REI-spect. It is from this position that we take time to clear our minds, to get prepared to learn and practice the art. It is from this stance that we show REI-spect to the heritage of Wado Ryu (Master Otsuka), to our instructors (who pass on what they have learned over the years, and to each other (as we work together and not against each other). Musubi Dachi is what we start our katas with and what we end our katas. It is the stance that we begin techniques and the stance that we start and end kumite (free style sparring).

HEIKO DACHI (Ready Stance)

With the command of Yoi (open), we enter in the ready stance. Heiko means *parallel*. To get into this foundational stance you move your left foot over as you close your fist, and then move the right foot over as you close your fist. Your fists are down and in front of you. If you take your right foot and turn it towards the left foot, that should be a good width for your parallel stance.

You have gone from Musubi Dachi, where you are in preparation, to Heiko Dachi, where you are ready for anything. Your eyes are open. Your peripheral vision is alert. Your body is relaxed but slightly tense, ready for the next command from your teacher - or if you are in the street or just experiencing life in general, you are ready for anything that comes your way. This is the stance you will be in as you prepare to run your alive kata, or when you get ready to do technique or kumite (free style sparring).

KIBA DACHI (Horse Stance)

This is one of those stances that you don't necessarily fight out of, but it is a great stance to practice techniques from as you develop leg strength. When you get into a deep horse stance, you look like you are riding a horse. If you are comfortable in this stance, you are doing it wrong. Sometimes our stances are merely practice stances.

ZENKUTSU DACHI (Fighting Stance)

This is the first of many fighting stances we learn. Zen (front) Kutsu (bent) Dachi (stance), is used to develop strength and must be done with a low center of gravity. It is long and narrow in nature, but is conducive to throwing many different kicks and punches depending for the need of the moment. Kicks can be thrown off of the front leg or off of the back leg. It is also utilized to practice floor techniques as we go up and down the floor with various kicks, punches, hand techniques, etc.

In my walk as a Christian, I've discovered foundation is everything. As in karate, without a good foundation everything else that we attempt will crumble - especially when the trials, troubles and tribulations of this world come against us. It is not a question of *if* we are going to face troubles. It's merely a matter of *when* they will come. When they come, we better be ready with a sure foundation.

"Everyone who comes to Me (Jesus), and hears My words, and acts upon them, I will show you whom he is like; he is like a man building a house, who dug deep and laid a foundation upon the rock; and when a flood arose, the river burst against that house and could not shake it, because it had been well built. But the one who has heard, and has not acted accordingly, is like a man who built a house upon the ground without any foundation; and the river burst against it and immediately it collapsed, and the ruin of that house was great."

Luke 6:47-49

It does not matter whether it is karate or Christianity, foundation is essential to both. As Bruce Cockburn sang in his song, **Lovers in a Dangerous Time**, *Nothing worth having comes without some kind of fight/ Got to kick at the darkness 'til it bleeds daylight.*

Well if you are going to kick in karate you better have a firm foundation. If you are going to do spiritual warfare and kick at the darkness (the devil) till it bleeds daylight, you better have a firm foundation.

"For we are God's fellow-workers; you are God's field, God's building. According to the grace of God which was given to me, as a wise master builder I laid a foundation, and another is building upon it. But let each man be careful how he builds upon it. For no man can lay a foundation other than the one which is laid, which is Jesus Christ."

I Corinthians 3:9-11

The foundation of this thing called the Kingdom of God is not meat or drink (eating or drinking), but righteousness, peace, and joy in the Holy Spirit. (Romans 14:17) The connect point for our stances in karate and our stances in the Kingdom are quite similar. Here is a definition from *Strong's Exhaustive Concordance of the Bible* (public domain) taken from my E-Sword.

KINGDOM: Basileia (bas-il-I'-ah) properly royalty, that is, (abstractly) rule, or (concretely) a realm (literally or figuratively): - kingdom, + reign. basileus (bas-il-yooce') (through the notion of a foundation of power); a sovereign (abstractly, relatively or figuratively): - king. basis (bas'-ece)=From βαίνω baino (to walk); a pace ("base"), that is, (by implication) THE FOOT: - foot.

Both karate and the kingdom must have a sure footing and foundation. The "foundation of power" is found in proper footing for both.

POSTURE

The next level on our pyramid paradigm is posture. We have a firm foundation which goes from the ground to the feet to the legs and hips. Posture goes from the hips to the top of our heads, which in turn affects everything from the top of the head to the ground. I well remember my mother and other adults, including teachers, who told me to "sit up" and to "quit slouching." In the work place, many spinal problems are attributed to poor posture as our work stations and seating are often ergonomically incorrect. These problems do not happen all at once, but if certain actions are done over and over again they become second nature with us. That is when we develop everything from carpal tunnel syndrome to cervical disc problems.

When we begin to throw techniques from an improper foundation, the technique is compromised by our posture. No matter how powerful the technique, poor posture can rob it of the power.

When you are in a good foundational stance - imagine, if you will, a pole going from the top of your head, through the body and straight down into the ground - the hips can turn, the stance remains secure, but your body is not bent over. Your body is upright and moving down the floor as one unit. Another aspect of this posture is your head. If your head is looking down, that is where your techniques will be aimed. It is good to remember that your enemy is not on the ground but in front of you.

Here is an interesting interchange between Bruce Lee and a student in the movie *Enter the Dragon*:

Lee: [*a student approaches Lee; both bow*] Kick me.
[*Student looks confused*]
Lee: Kick me.
[*Student attempts kick*]
Lee: What was that? An Exhibition? We need emotional content. Now try again!
[*Student tries again*]
Lee: I said "emotional content." Not anger! Now try again!
[*Student tries again and succeeds*]
Lee: That's it! How did it feel?
[*Student thinks; Lee smacks his head*]
Lee: Don't think. *Feel*. It's like a finger pointing at the moon.
[*Looks at student who is looking at the finger; smacks student again*]
Lee: Do not concentrate on the finger or you will miss all of the heavenly glory!
[*Student bows; Lee smacks him again*]
Lee: Never take your eyes off your opponent - even when you're bowing!

[*Student bows again this time keeping his eyes on Lee*]
<u>Lee</u>: That's better.

My wife, Brenda, and I love this interchange where Lee smacks the student on the head. The idea is keep your focus; keep your eyes on your opponent and do not be distracted. Ever since that movie came out in the early 70s, Brenda and I will periodically smack each other on the forehead.

In karate, I had to be told more than once to get my eyes up, that the enemy was not down there. Chin up; eyes open; body straight; foundation solid. It makes all the difference in the world as to how I through a technique. If your body is leaning, and if your knee is pointed downward, guess where your kick will land. Your kicks can often be higher by merely utilizing proper posture; getting your knee up and then delivering the technique. So it is with life.

It is Sensei Taylor's custom during the belt exams, after the new belts have been tied around the recipients' waists, to go down the line and shake their hands. If the recipient is a white belt going to a gold belt, and it is their first exam, they tend to look down at the ground. Mr. Taylor tells them, "Look up into my eyes." That is a big part of their karate training.

Proper posture (body, head, eye contact) elevates you from someone who can be picked on at school to someone who can't be bullied.

When the Apostle Paul was encouraging his son in the faith, Timothy, he gave him a lesson in holding his head up and not hanging it down in fear.

"And for this reason I remind you to kindle afresh the gift of God which is in you through the laying on of my hands. For God has not given us a spirit of fear (timidity), but of power, love and a sound mind."

II Timothy 1:6-7

That spirit of fear that Paul is talking about is a spirit of timidity - of being afraid of man. I have learned in karate that we need not fear anyone, but look them straight in the eyes .and meet them head on, whether in shaking a hand or fighting them on the street. The Greek word for power is *dunamis*, which means *dynamic ability*. We have been given a dynamic ability to face our fears. Love is that agape, God kind of love that motivates us, and a sound mind is a mind that is not distracted by fear. When we combine in karate our dynamic ability, love and respect for others with clear thinking we can accomplish much.

I like the classic rock song by the band, Argent, that encourages us to *Hold your head up, hold your head up, Hold your head up/ hold your head high!*

TECHNIQUE

The third and final component to our pyramid analogy, technique, is ready to be implemented. We are now ready to throw proper kicks, punches and blocks. The foundation is sure, the posture is upright, the eyes are straight ahead, but just because you have a good foundation and your posture is in order, does not mean that you automatically are able to throw the perfect technique. You can have the first two down pat, but still throw sloppy technique.

For example, one of the first kicks you learn is a Mai Geri (Front Kick). When you first try to throw this kick it will either look like someone kicking a football or a walking horse plodding its hoofs along. The steps to a good Mai Geri would be:
(1) turn you front heel in
(2) lift you knee up to where you could sit a glass of water on you leg
(3) extend the leg straight out

(4) bring the leg back on the same trajectory that it went out

(5) place the foot either back in the same stance you started or gently place your foot in front of you.

If you are throwing the technique of a Jun Zuki (moving forward front punch) you would:

(1) be in a good Zenkutzu Dachi (fighting stance)

(2) posture low and upright

(3) begin to move forward

(4) as you move forward have your front fist that is out begin to come back as your back fist trades places

(5) the fists should pass by each other about the same time

(6) as the back fist becomes the front fist, the front fist becomes the back fist

(7) the back fist is now in a good hikite (pulling hand) palm up.

(8) all fist are closed properly.

All of this comes with much practice as you begin to run the techniques without even thinking about them. But even after years of practice you still learn something that you might never have thought about. This thing called practice is a lifestyle. If I am going to walk out my Christian life, I must live it with passion.

"For to me to live is Christ, and to die is gain."

Philippians 1:21

Whether I am practicing technique or practicing my Christianity, it must be with passion.

"Only conduct yourselves in a manner worthy of the Gospel of Christ; so that whether I come and see you or remain absent, I may hear of you that you are standing firm in one spirit, with one mind, striving together for the faith of the Gospel."

Philippians 1:27

"So then, my beloved, just as you always obeyed, not as in my presence only, but now much more in my absence, work out your own salvation with fear and trembling; for it is God who is at work in you, both to will and to work for His good pleasure."

Philippians 2:12-13

This passage is not encouraging us to come up with some new method of salvation, but to work out *practically* how we live out our faith. It's like our karate kata and technique, which has generations of tradition on how to do them; but *we work out our own kata, our own technique*, to make it ours. We don't change it but we do make it alive.

Well, there you have it. Foundation, posture and technique. Just another lesson that I learned in the dojo, that extends beyond the dojo, into my world.

CHAPTER GO (FIVE)
PERSEVERANCE
Hanging In There Like A Bitin' Sow

PERSEVERANCE: proskarterēsis (*pros-kar-ter'-ay-sis*); *persistency:* - perseverance. proskartereō (*pros-kar-ter-eh'-o*) - to *be earnest towards,* that is, (to a thing) to *persevere, be constantly* diligent, or (in a place) to *attend* assiduously all the exercises, or (to a person) to *adhere* closely *to* (as a servitor): - attend (give self) continually (upon), continue (in, instant in, with), wait on (continually).

One thing that you will *not* survive without at the dojo is perseverance. It is that characteristic that keeps you keeping on even when you don't want to keep on. Many times on the journey for the black belt, I felt like giving up. My body, my mind, my emotions, my friends all screamed, "Give up!" Leg cramps, multiple torn rotator cuff injuries, knee injuries and surgery all offered perfect excuses for giving up.

What kept me going on? What lessons was I learning that compelled me on to the completion of the task?

I was anchored to my dream. I never lost sight of my desire to get my black belt. If you remember why you started, it will go a long way to keeping you on the *"the road you started traveling on."* (*Keep On Walking* by Dogwood)

I was traveling the road with someone else who had the same desires. Encouragement from my fellow karatekas (fellow students) got me through the hard times more than once.

My instructors always knew how to push and encourage me at the same time. They always brought out the best in me even when only they could see the best.

Little pieces of electrical tape wrapped around the end of the belt, showing that I was one step closer was like the proverbial carrot dangling before me.

Reaching the next level by testing and getting a new belt wrapped around my waist was a mile marker for me.

There is the element of tenacity in this thing called perseverance. I love the picture of the stork who is swallowing a frog. There are various versions of this picture but they all have the same theme. A stork has a frog in its mouth. The only problem is, the frog has its little hands around the stork's neck, refusing to go down. For me the best thing about the pictures I've seen is the look of utter surprise in the eyes of the stork. Underneath the picture is the caption, "Never Give Up," or sometimes, "Never Quit."

Sensei Taylor has told us more than once, "The only reason you will *not* get your black belt, is *if* you stop coming." The great *if* is perseverance. Perseverance is hinged on our choice to keep on in the face of adversity. At any time on the rocky road of my journey, I could have quit. I could have rationalized, justified, manipulate facts and emotions into my way out. I could have reached the maximum amount of pressure that I could stand and just not come back to class. At any given moment I could have walked off the dojo floor and out the door. I could have taken offense at something my instructors said to me, as a source of motivation, and used it as and excuse to stop coming.

It has been said, "Anything worth having is worth the fight." (Unknown) It's worth repeating the earlier quote from the Bruce Cockburn song "Lovers in a Dangerous Time."

But nothing worth having comes without some kind of fight/ Got to kick at the darkness 'til it bleeds daylight

The continual kicking (action on our part) at the darkness (the obstacle) until (the perseverance factor) it (the darkness) bleeds daylight (desired result). If you stop kicking because of the overwhelming darkness, you will remain in the darkness. If you keep on keeping on kicking against what is standing against you, or is in your way, or is your excuse, there will eventually be a crack in the darkness. Streams of light will begin to pierce your darkness until it floods our lives with sunlight, like dawn breaking through the darkness of the night with a new day. Every time I kept on executing a Mai Geri (front kick), even when I did not want to be in class, even when my mind said *kick* and my leg said *walk*, each time I executed imperfect technique I, in essence, was persevering, kicking at the darkness of my desire to quit until it bled the daylight of not giving up.

These principles, these lessons that I have learned on the floor of the dojo, translate into the life we live in the land called *Nitty Gritty*. No, real life is not a movie or a television show where pain is not felt by the audience, where problems are wrapped up between commercials. There is a reason it is called *real* life. Real life has real obstacles, but there are also real opportunities not to quit but to persevere. As you may have noticed, these principles have been established and underscored in my walk as a Christian. In the transition from law to grace, from John the Baptist to Jesus, there was the need for perseverance and tenacity because life is not easy.

"Truly, I say to you, among those born of women there has not arisen anyone greater than John the Baptist; yet he who is least in the kingdom of heaven is greater than he. And from the days of John the Baptist until

now the kingdom of heaven suffers violence (forcibly entered), and violent men take it by force (seize it for themselves)."

Matthew 11:11-12

In his book, "Think and Grow Rich," author Napoleon Hill states, "Truly thoughts are things, and powerful things at that, when they are mixed with definiteness of purpose, persistence, and a burning desire for their translation into riches, or other material objects." Perseverance, or persistence, is one of the driving forces that I had for a black belt. My burning desire began with my thoughts. I did not have random thoughts of anything but the prize. When my body and emotions were crying out quit, the burning desire and definiteness of purpose was empowered by my persistence. My perseverance was rooted in my vision for the black belt. At the end, when it was especially hard to keep on keeping on, in my mind I already had a black belt around my waist. It was only a matter of not giving up.

At Bill Taylor's Bushido School of Karate we are evaluated by belt exams. We go through the process of 11 examinations. It gives us an opportunity to practice for the Wado Federation Examination. Sensei Taylor says each time, that in a sense these exams do not matter. Only one examination really matters - and that is the black belt exam.

Keep your eye on the prize and persevere.

CHAPTER ROKU (SIX)
THE PINAN CONNECTION
Basic Peaceful Mind

PEACE: shalôm shalôm (*shaw-lome', shaw-lome'*); SAFE, that is, (figuratively) *well, happy, friendly*; also (abstractly) *welfare*, that is, health, prosperity, peace: shalam (*shaw-lam'*)=A primitive root; to *be safe* (in mind, body or estate); figuratively to *be* (causatively *make*) *completed*; by implication to *be friendly*; by extension to *reciprocate* (in various applications

PEACE: eirēnē (*i-rah'-nay*)=Probably from a primary verb εἰρω eiro (to *join*); *peace* (literally or figuratively); by implication *prosperity*: - one, peace, quietness, rest, + set at one again.

"The steadfast of mind, Thou will keep in perfect peace, because it is stayed on Thee."

Isaiah 26:3

In a world filled with unrest, there is a real, basic need, for a peaceful mind on the dojo floor of Wado Ryu -The Way of Peace/Harmony. I have learned lessons on how to practice in peace and not unrest.

The core of Wado Ryu Karate, the center point, the spine, the backbone of this art that I study is found in a series of five katas known as The Pinans. There are five Pinan katas in the series including:

(1) Pinan Nidan
(2) Pinan Shodan
(3) Pinan Sandan

(4) Pinan Yondan
(5) Pinan Godan

Each of these katas brings something new to the table. Each one has a particular theme or themes, that we build upon as we learn them. On every examination that I have taken, the Pinan kata's were on there. The higher the belt exam, the greater the number of Pinans I would be expected to run. One thing you can be sure of when you take your black belt exam - you will run all five Pinans. We are encouraged to practice the Pinans daily.

The word *Pinan* can mean either *basic* or *peaceful mind* (a state of relaxation and ease). I have found that in karate, you can only run an alive kata if you have a peaceful mind, in the state of relaxation and ease. It is basic to an alive kata. If your mind is at unrest - in a state of tension, trying too hard - the kata will reflect the inner you. The lesson learned as applied to everyday life is; as you attempt to run an alive life (aka abundant life), the basic concept is to run your life from a state of relaxation and ease.

In each Pinan Kata new techniques are introduced regarding stances, angles, concepts and movements. As we progress through the Pinans we build upon previous lessons learned with certain moves incorporated in other katas (after we learn the first two Pinans). This will bring us to another discipline that we must master - concentrate. As we do a move from Pinan Yondan, we must concentrate so when we run a later kata like Ku San Ku, we don't end up running Pinan Yondan instead of running Ku San Ku. Again - "Ain't that life?"

PINAN NIDAN

Although *Ni* means *two*, it is the first Pinan we learn. Up to this point we have learned First and Second Basic Kata, which have nice, easy, straight-forward linear moves. In

Pinan Nidan we are now introduced to a new stances, new concepts, new angles and new perspectives.

The first new technique is Otoshi. This is where we use dropping of body weight to generate power. It is more than just taking a fist and dropping it on someone. That generates some limited power, but when your entire body weight drops that power is maximized.

In Sensei Taylor's book, "Wado Ryu: A Fighter's Perspective," he states, "Otoshi is sometimes referred to as the utilization of potential energy."

In life, we all have this potential energy that we can drop on obstacles that try to stand in our way, obstacles that try to prevent us from accomplishing our purposes. Maximizing the power potential can be the difference between winning or losing.

The other new technique that we learn is Irimi. Irimi mean to enter an area or space. Not only do we enter into an area or space, we also avoid an attack by the shifting of our bodies from a front view and with the twist of the body. Back in the seventies we were taught that in the olden days of karatem Irimi, the entering in, was entering within the body cavity physically to pull out internal organs. Yikes! If someone comes swinging a ball bat or 2 X 4 piece of lumber at your head, the natural reflex is to pull back to avoid getting hit. I don't know, but I have heard that the power generated from the swinging bat is more damaging at the tip of the bat versus the handle of the bat. Irimi can help you as you enter in to the space of the arm area and diffuse the power by hitting various areas in the arm and shoulder area utilizing a source block. Once you enter in you have access to other body parts to attack.

In our everyday lives we try to back up to avoid getting hurt (which is not a bad thing), but sometimes we have to face our fears and enter in to prevent further attacks.

PINAN SHODAN

This pinan kata introduced the concept of double movement - performing one technique while at the same time executing another movement. Aaaaah...kata multitasking!

In the classes that I have taken over the years, and the various books that I have read on this concept of double movement, the twisting of the body is the key principle. According to "Karate Katas of Wado Ryu," by Shingo Ohgami, during punches, blocks and other techniques, "...the body is twisted in the same direction as the punch itself. But in double moment the body is twisted in the other direction than the technique itself."

The Pinan concept of peaceful mind, the state of relaxation and ease, is the only way this concept of double moment/movement will ever become fluid in our techniques.

In our physical and spiritual lives, specifically in our relationships with God, we are faced with a multitude of situations, circumstances, people, etc. We have to juggle multiple emotions and tasks. I have found myself more than once in what I've heard called, "The Juggle of the Struggle." Many times as I am trying to juggle one thing, I drop the other thing. Then I become so not at ease, and so not relaxed, and oh so not at one with myself - which only complicates an already frustrating situation.

I like what Sensei Taylor wrote in his book, "Wado Ryu: A Fighter's Perspective."

"This double movement lends a unique snap to the end of the technique." Another quote from Sensei Taylor is, "Fighting is a game of adjustments."

In the Struggle of the Juggle we are faced with constant changes coming at us, and if we don't adjust, the struggle wins. As in sparring (kumite) you can't get into the same rhythm of doing the same technique over and over without expecting your opponent to begin to read you, adjust and counter against you. If you just constantly block and never throw a technique, you may never get hit (which ain't bad), but you will never overcome and triumph. Double movement gives you great opportunity to block and then counter.

PINAN SANDAN

This next Pinan introduces the concept of small single movements; or more specifically power in small moves. In this kata the body twisting is back to the direction the technique is thrown. In boxing and kickboxing there is a *squared circle* that two opponents are able to move around in and throw kicks, punches, spinning techniques. But from my observation, a lot of the action takes place in closed off areas in the corners or against the ropes. Muhammed Ali (aka Cassius Clay) perfected what he called the *Rope-a-Dope* technique. He drew his opponent in, and as he covered up they expended energy trying to penetrate his physical fortress. Then, in an up-close proximity, he could counter. You can see many a fighter always trying to close off the ring and back the opponent into the corner where they can work their opponent over. In these situations, instead of wide shots or spinning kicks, the small movements - or better said, the power in those small movements - can be very effective.

In real life, if we are confronted by someone who is trying to hurt us, it might not be in spacious environment. It will more likely be in an enclosed area, in a crowded space or our backs against the wall. You might not have the luxury of delivering a spinning kick. You might not have plenty of room to throw some other technique. But front/back arm burn blocks (uchi/ude uke) can be utilized, or a short vertical punch (tate) can be executed, or elbow strikes (empi) can be effective tools in your powerful small moves.

How many of us have at one time in our life, have had our backs against the wall?

The enemy of want and need may be breathing down our necks. The economy, sickness, disease, world events, gloom and doom may be the front page news taking place around the world, but it looms even larger in our own homes.

PINAN YONDAN

This kata introduces the concepts of Jujitsu. You might remember that the Mr. Moto movies were the catalyst for my love for the martial arts. He used jujitsu instead of guns to defeat the enemy. The roots of Wado Ryu were birth in Master Otsuka's roots in sword and jujitsu. I have never met Master Otsuka, but I have seen many pictures and videos of him in action with swords, jujitsu and actually running the Pinan katas. He was a small, frail looking man. On the surface you would think he would break if you touched him, but he presents himself with gentle but powerful presence. To be able to control a situation by the mere twist of the wrist, the shifting of the hips, the reaping with a leg sweep is an amazing thing to watch. To take advantage of your opponent's momentum, weight, imbalance can mean the difference between death and survival.

In our everyday lives, many times we are faced with insurmountable odds that are coming at us with an intensity designed to destroy us. Dojo lessons teach us how to not take the brunt of the impact, but to shift, adjust and use what means harm for us and turn it to our advantage for our good. We don't deny the reality of the circumstance, but as we counter-attack, we deny the right of that reality to rule our lives.

When Joseph, the dreamer, told his dreams to his brothers they became very jealous. They plotted against him, faked his death, threw him into a pit, lied to their father about him and sold him into slavery. (Genesis 37:1-36) What transpired was a series of events that, on the surface, at times looked bad and at times looked good. Sometimes it looked like God was nowhere to be found. At other times it looked like He had everything covered. At one point Joseph was elevated to a place of power in Egypt (the place where he was sold into slavery). He was a position to get even with his brothers.

When the brothers realized that the one who controlled their fate was their brother, the one they betrayed, they were justifiably afraid for their lives. But Joseph countered their fear with this statement, *"Do not be afraid. For am I in God's place?"* (Genesis 50:19) Joseph then followed up with another twist and declared, *"And as for you, you meant evil against me, but God meant it for good, in order to bring about this present result to preserve many people alive."* (Genesis 50:20)

So it is with life, when we are attacked, thrown a curve ball, overwhelmed by the enormity of our emotional opponents. Instead of fighting with fear, we can learn the Yon Dan lesson and counter with a throw, a side step, a countermove - jujitsu-style - and speak love into the situation or look at it from another perspective.

Joseph took control and instead of vengeance countered with love. He told them, *"So therefore, do not be afraid. I will provide for you and your little ones. So he comforted them and spoke kindly to them."* (Genesis 50:21) Now that is a counter-throw that will get their attention.

PINAN GODAN

The final Pinan kata in the series is the fifth one or Go (five) Dan. The concept for this kata is avoidance of a staff or swords being swung at your legs or your body. In Godan we see some jumping (as if over a bo staff being swung at your feet and legs) and an introduction of kokutsu dachi - a leaning back away from an object.

In this kata there are two places that are critical that you must move forward. If you don't move forward it will mess up the rest of the kata. During one of my examinations, for the life of me I could not remember this kata. I got to a certain place and my mind would draw a blank. This can be embarrassing when all eyes are upon you, and you are asked to redo the kata three times. (This also happened to me while running Nihanchi, but that's another story.)

What got me through this kata during that exam was Senpai Mike Wilson (who I consider a major mentor and source of encouragement during my karate journey) as he casually walked by me and whispered into my ear, "Go forth in Godan." When I heard those words, it clicked. And I went forth - and the rest of the kata fell in to place.

Sometimes in real life, when we feel as if our lives are in limbo, we just need the whisper of a friend to encourage us to keep on keeping on, to go forth, to not give up, to never quit. I love the 23rd Psalm as it speaks of walking through the valley of the shadow of death. The Psalmist states, *"Yea, even though I walk through the valley of the shadow of death, I fear no evil, for Thou art with me. Thy rod and Thy staff, they comfort me."*

Psalm 23:4

(NOTE: This is one of the only references where I am mentioned in the Bible along with my office crew: Thy *Rod* and Thy *Staff*.)

The key lesson in Godan is the forward walk. Notice that the Psalmist is *walking through* the valley of the shadow of death; not stopping, but going forth. The old saying is, "If you keep on walking (going forth) through the valley of the shadow of death, you will eventually come out the other side."

As with all of the other Pinan katas, the concept of using all of the specific and individual techniques learned with a peaceful mind, in a state of relaxation and ease, will get you through the various attacks, oppositions and schemes plotted against you in your real life.

CHAPTER SICHI (SEVEN)
BREATHE AND RELAX

"Relax."

- Sensei Bill Herzer

"Breath."

- Senpai Mike Wilson

When you are in an examination, there is a tendency to get very tense, uptight, nervous, anxious, distracted and definitely *not* relaxed. As you are kicking, punching, running kata and moving up and down the floor with six Black Belt examiners looking at your every move, relaxation is the farthest thing from your mind. As a matter of fact the tendency is to get even more tense. This tension affects every thing that you are doing, from technique to muscle control to breathing. More than once I have had instructors not only say "Relax," but "Breath."

More than once an instructor has come up behind me and pressed my shoulders down as they whispered in my ears, "Relax." More than once I moved down the floor throwing moving forward front punches (junzuki), and when I stopped the instructor would push down on my arm, only to met a resistance tighter than a piece of wood coming out of my arm socket. More than once would I try to throw a front jab and it was slower than molasses during winter during a deep freeze. Why, oh why was there such tightness and slowness in my techniques? Because I was not relaxed.

Various dictionaries define "Relax" as:

Verb (used with object)
(1) to make less tense, rigid, or firm; make lax: to relax the muscles.
(2) to diminish the force of.
(3) to slacken or abate, as effort, attention, etc.
(4) to make less strict or severe, as rules, discipline, etc.: *to relax the requirements for a license.*
(5) to release or bring relief from the effects of tension, anxiety, etc.: *A short swim always relaxes me.*

Verb (used without object)
(6) to become less tense, rigid, or firm.
(7) to become less strict or severe; grow milder.
(8) to reduce or stop work, effort, application, etc., especially for the sake of rest or recreation.
(9) to release oneself from inhibition, worry, tension, etc.

"Breath" is defined as:

Noun
(1) the air inhaled and exhaled in respiration.
(2) respiration, especially as necessary to life.
(3) life; vitality.
(4) the ability to breathe easily and normally: *She stopped to regain her breath.*
(5) time to breathe; pause or respite: *Give him a little breath*
(6) a single inhalation or respiration: *He took a deep breath*
(7) the brief time required for a single respiration; a moment or instant: *They gave it to her and took it away all in a breath.*
(8) a slight suggestion, hint, or whisper: *The breath of slander never touched her.*
(9) a light current of air.

In Shingo Ohgami's classic book "Karate Katas of Wado Ryu," he talks about the need for "relaxation before and after the motion." Every move that we make - big, little, reflexive or purposeful - is based on the contraction of our muscles. There is an electrical stimulation with the cause and effect being the contraction of the muscle. The problem comes when the muscle is "tensed already in the original stage." Sensei Ohgami goes on to point out how if the muscle is tense already, then it must relax and then contract again to throw the technique. If you throw a technique and then relax, the next technique will not have to relax from the tense (non-relaxed position) to initiate the next contraction. This eliminates one step, going from three steps (tense, relaxed, contraction) to two steps (relax, contraction), making for a quicker technique.

Senpai Mike Wilson regularly tells people, "Control your breathing and don't let your breathing control you." To do this you don't just gasp for air, but you take deep breaths into your nostrils down into your lungs, hold that breath for a few seconds, then release through your mouth. It is amazing how more controlled your breathing is, and how quickly you can recover. Knowing the concept is easy. Doing it, particularly when you are in the need for oxygen, is harder. Thus, your instructor comes up to your side and says, "Breeeeeeeeeath." And another instructor comes up from the other side and says, "Relax."

Breathing and relaxation are the two keys to performance in karate - and in every other sport as well as in every day, nitty-gritty, in-your-face life. How many times are you faced with very tense, anxious moments and you find yourself so tight that you can't focus or think?

The Bible speaks a lot about breathing and relaxation.

"Therefore humble yourselves under the mighty hand of God, that He may exalt you at the proper time, casting all your anxiety on Him, because He cares for you."

I Peter 5:6-7

"Be anxious for nothing, but in everything by prayer, supplication with thanksgiving let/allow your request be made known to God. And the peace of God which surpasses all comprehension will guard your hearts and your minds in Christ Jesus."

Philippians 4:6-7

The act of humbling yourself is bringing yourself into a state of relaxation as you know that God is with you in the midst of your distractions. Peace will replace tension. When you are in a relaxed, peaceful mode, you can execute the techniques of life with one less step to be involved, as in the Ohgami example.

Breath is important in the spiritual process of life. During the creation of man, the first case of CPR was administered. God *breathed* His *breath* into the nostrils of a lump of clay, and the cause and effect was *Life!* (Genesis 2:7)

BREATHED: nâphach *(naw-fakh')*=A primitive root; to *puff,* in various applications (literally, to *inflate, blow* hard, *scatter, kindle, expire*; figuratively, to *disesteem*): - blow, breath, give up, cause to lose [life], seething, snuff.

BREATH: nᵉshâmâh *(nesh-aw-maw')*= a *puff,* that is, *wind,* angry or vital *breath,* divine *inspiration, intellect* or (concretely) an *animal:* - blast, (that) breath (-eth), inspiration, soul, spirit.

This thing called *Breath* and *Relax* is seen in Isaiah 40:28-31. If you need strength and renewal, here is the key. During my 2nd Degree Black Belt Examination, I wrote these verses on an index card and placed it on the inside of my uniform. Of course it fell out, but every time that I passed by the card on the floor I gained breath and strength to complete the task that I was smack dab in the middle of at the time.

"Do you not know? Have you not heard? The Everlasting God, the Lord, the Creator of the ends of the earth, does not become weary or tired. His understanding is inscrutable. He gives strength to the weary, and to him who lacks might He increases power. Though youths grow weary and tired, and vigorous young men stumble badly. Yet those who wait for the LORD (relax and breath) will mount up with wings like eagles, they will run and not get tired, they will walk and not become weary."

Isaiah 40:28-31

WAIT: qâvâh (*kaw-vaw'*)=A primitive root; to *bind* together (perhaps by *twisting*), that is, *collect*; (figuratively) to *expect:* - gather (together), look, patiently, tarry, wait (for, on, upon).

RENEW: châlaph (*khaw-laf'*)=A primitive root; properly to *slide* by, that is, (by implication) to *hasten* away, *pass* on, *spring* up, *pierce* or *change:* - abolish, alter change, cut off, go on forward, grow up, be over, pass (away, on, through), renew, sprout, strike through.

STRENGTH: kôach kôach (*ko'-akh, ko'-akh*)=From an unused root meaning to *be firm*; *vigor*, literally (*force*, in a good or a bad sense) or figuratively (*capacity, means, produce*); also (from its hardiness) a large *lizard:* - ability, able, chameleon, force, fruits, might, power (-ful), strength, substance, wealth.

When you are moving up and down the dojo floor of life, relax. Breath.

CHAPTER HACHI (EIGHT)
THE INTENTION

When I started studying the art of karate (empty hand) back in 2001, I was given a uniform and the Student Guide. I found that the Student Guide would be a valuable tool and guidebook on my journey. Within the Student Guide was the Mission Statement for the school, a welcome letter from the owner (Sensei Taylor), rules of the school, policies and procedures, information on the Black Belt Club, Leadership Team Benefits, Belt Curriculum (with English and Japanese terminology), sparring rules and much, much more. One thing that stood out to me, was The Student Creed. The notation on the creed was "Students must memorize, strive to understand and live out the tenets of The Student Creed on a daily basis."

The Student Creed has three parts:

(1) I INTEND to develop myself
In a positive manner and
Avoid anything that would reduce
my mental growth or physical health

(2) I INTEND to develop self discipline
in order to bring out the best
in myself and others

(3) I INTEND to use
what skills I learn in class
constructively and defensively

to help myself and my fellow man
and never be abusive or offensive

For our purposes, the word *creed* is defined as any system or codification of belief or opinion. This belief system is something that we can look back to on our journey to keep us on the road that we travel. In the dojo, the creed sets us apart from a bunch of thugs learning how to destroy things and maim people with our hands and feet. The true student is in a learning process with these goals in mind. Let us look at the intentions of the student.

STUDENT CREED BREAKDOWN

The two words common to all three sections of the creed are I INTEND. As we look at each section we will be looking at the intention of the student. We will now break down the Creed - word for word, thought for thought, intention for intention.

STUDENT CREED SECTION ONE

I: This speaks of the individual nature of this art. While there are opportunities to compete with others, the bottom line is that you are only competing with yourself. Only you can practice. Only you are kicking, punching, running kata. It does not matter what anyone else is doing on the dojo floor, other than encouraging you to be your best. You are making this thing called *karate* a personal thing.

INTEND: Intention is something that you plan to do. It is not just some happenstance event. You do it on purpose. It is planned. The old saying is that "the road is paved with good intentions." But many times people either never started or their best laid plans, like those of mice and men, tend to fail. Our intentions are not some New Year Resolutions, but desire manifested in hard work to completion.

TO DEVELOP: Development is a progressive event. It has a beginning, it has a progression and it has an ending. In between the beginning and the ending are the things that you do, the building process where you take the plan, where you take the blueprint, where you take the curriculum of the school and work and build and develop it to your desired result.

MYSELF: This goes back to the beginning when I declared, "I intend…" Me, myself and I are the focus of this declaration. Others may be involved in the process, but only I can make the choice to do what is needed to accomplish my intentions.

IN A POSITIVE MANNER: *Positive* is the attitude, and *manner* is the way that you do something. A negative attitude attracts negative results. If the way, or manner, that you approach life is negative, you will derail your intentions and purpose and nothing will ever develop in your life except negativity. You will repel any positive influences.

AND AVOID ANYTHING THAT WOULD REDUCE: As we walk in this world there are thousands of opportunities to reduce our desired results. As in Wado Ryu, the ability to avoid a kick or a punch can determine the success of the conflict. You don't need an exaggerated avoidance, just the subtle shifting of the body. I like the advice of a father to a son in the book of Pro-Verbs (the book of Positive Action): *"My son, if sinners entice you…do not consent."* The next word that jumps out is *anything*. Whether it is drugs or negative people, avoid them. Negative will suck you dry and reduce your potential.

MY MENTAL GROWTH: Your mental growth is how you *think*. Zig Ziglar describes negative mental growth as "stinking thinking." In the Sunday school class I teach, called

The Ruminator Sunday School Class, we describe it this way: "Unrestrained thoughts (what we think), produces unrestrained words (what we say), resulting in unrestrained actions (what we do)." What you feed your mind will determine how you grow mentally. The Apostle Paul writes about how the mind can affect the anxiety in our lives.

"Finally brethren, whatever is true, whatever is honorable, whatever is right, whatever is pure, whatever is lovely, whatever is of good report, if there is any excellence, and if anything worthy of praise, let/allow your mind to dwell on these things."

Philippians 4:8

OR PHYSICAL HEALTH: This can be anything from sleep deprivation to detrimental things we allow into our bodies such as drugs, alcohol, tobacco smoke, etc. What you allow into your body will affect you in a positive way or a negative way. Notice that the mind and the body, while separate, cannot be totally separated. What you think affects your body, especially if you allow worry, fear, tension, anxiety, doubt and unbelief to dominate you. Your physical being, your body, is related to your stamina, flexibility and your weight. I battle with all of these, and unless I avoid certain things my mental and physical health will be out of control

STUDENT CREED SECTION TWO

I: Again, it is your individual choice.

INTEND: Your personal purpose - that is your personal focus.

TO DEVELOP: A progressive plan.

SELF DISCIPLINE: Discipline has a bad rap and suffers from a negative connotation. Discipline is often perceived as either someone beating on you for your bad behavior, or you beating on yourself because you are trying to atone for you sins by punishing yourself. But true discipline is a positive thing.

Discipline: gumnazo¯ (*goom-nad'-zo*); to *practice naked* (in the games), that is, *train* (figuratively): - exercise. gumnos (*goom-nos'*)=Of uncertain affinity; *nude* (absolutely or relatively, literally or figuratively): - naked.

To practice naked is a reference to the Greek games where the athletes would remove their long flowing clothing so they would not be hindered or encumbered as they practiced. As martial artists, we need to remove whatever hinders our practice of the art. The prime time of the removal of our mental encumbrances is as we bow in Rei-spect in our attention stance, leave the day's work, problems, frustrations, fears and anxieties behind, and focus on the task at hand.

In I Timothy 4:7 the Apostle Paul is encouraging his son in the faith, Timothy, to discipline himself for the purpose of godliness.

Nobody is going to discipline you, in godliness or karate, except you. Nobody is going to follow you home from the dojo to make sure that you are practicing your kata, technique, cardio, etc. You must intend to develop self (the key word is *self*) discipline. The areas of discipline in my spiritual life are found in I Timothy 4:12. They include:

(1) Speech (what I say)
(2) Conduct (how I act)
(3) Love (what motivates me)
(4) Faith (what I believe)
(5) Purity (what I allow in my life)

IN ORDER: This points to the purpose for self discipline. According to I Timothy 4:7, the purpose of the discipline is godliness in the areas of speech, conduct, love, faith and purity.

TO BRING OUT THE BEST: In the process of making butter, cream rises to the top. For this to happen there must be agitation in the butter churn. So it is with bringing out the best in others; there must be purposeful action. Bringing out the best will not come from stagnation. It will not come from just reading about karate.

You can only bring out the best (tempered technique) by practice, and deal with the worst (purging sloppy techniques) by disciplined practice.

IN MYSELF: Before I can help others, I must help myself. But on the other hand, as you help others you will help yourself.

"In karate you can read about it, hear someone talking about it, see someone doing it - but unless you do it, by repetition (practice), you merely know about karate. The same applies for Christianity. Unless you do it, over and over again (practice), you only know about Christianity"

(R.L.B.)

When Jesus was questioned about the most important commandment, He responded by quoting Deuteronomy 6:4-5 and Leviticus 19:18 - *"And you shall love the Lord your God with all your heart, and with all your soul, and with all your mind, and with all your strength. The second is this, you shall love your neighbor as yourself. There is no other commandment greater than these."*
Mark 12:30, Luke 10:27, Matthew 22:37

In these passages we usually miss the part about loving your neighbor *as* ourselves. You can't love your neighbor *as yourself*, unless you first love your *self*.

AND IN OTHERS: I have found that what we learn about karate on the dojo floor is in turn passed down to the belts below us. We teach others what we have learned. This can occur all the way from the white belt to the black belt. I have found, as a teacher, that I learn from what I teach. I know that those advanced belts above me brought out the best in me. Something as simple as correcting a waving hand in Shuto Uke versus a strong block with the double movement can make the difference from a sloppy looking kata to a sharp kata.

I apply this tenet of the Student Creed in my everyday life, in my Christian walk and in my karate walk (or kick). In the book of Philippians, the Apostle Paul speaks of this attitude that Jesus had, and we are to have the same attitude in our lives.

"Do nothing from selfishness or empty conceit, but with humility of mind let each of you regard on another as more important than himself; do not merely look out for your own personal interests but also for the interests of others. Have this attitude in yourselves which was also in Christ Jesus."

Philippians 2:3-5

NOTE: Tenet #1 speaks of self development and tenet #2 carries that intended self development from you to others. Now we finish with tenet 3 of the Student Creed taking the skills that we have to our fellow man, wo-man, hu-man beings.

STUDENT CREED SECTION THREE

I: We continue with our personal intentions.

INTEND: An old saying goes, "Shoot for the stars; hit the moon." The idea is doing something on purpose with a goal in mind.

TO USE WHAT SKILLS I LEARN IN CLASS: This is where we take practical application outside of a school setting. This does not mean that we learn how to kick someone in the stomach (ore elsewhere) from the school, and carry that knowledge into the streets. If all you have learned is technique and not self control and the philosophy of Wanominchi (the way of peace and harmony) then you have missed the point. It's like learning how to live the Christian life, then going out into the world - away from the four walls of the church building - and condemning others because they are not like you.

CONSTRUCTIVELY: We should always constructively edify, or build up, other people.

EDIFY/BUILD UP: epoikodomeō (*ep-oy-kod-om-eh'-o*)= to *build upon*, that is, (figuratively) to *rear up:* - build thereon (thereupon, on, upon).

Even within the karate community you find people who still have *not* learned that it is not about being a bad ass and keeping others down by not being constructive, but being destructive. When you think about the words, "Wado Ryu," and the concept being the Way of Peace (and peace meaning to bring people back to a wholeness and rest), this goes along with being constructive.

AND DEFENSIVELY: The nature of self defense is - defending self. Defense is not just blocks. Blocks are important, but defense is the removal of the threat. Whether it is an attack in the alley or a verbal attack from another person, you do not just drop an atomic bomb when turning and walking away will diffuse the situation. Hopefully the skills you have learned in class .will translate to real life.

TO HELP MYSELF: If you can't love yourself you can't effectively love anyone else. Remember the chapter on REI-SPECT. As The Staple Singers sang, "Respect yourself, respect yourself If you don't respect yourself ain't nobody gonna give a good cahoot, na na na na. Respect yourself, respect yourself" Help yourself help others.

AND MY FELLOW MAN: Of course, this statement means man, wo-man and hu-man. The question has been asked, "Who is my neighbor?" The answer is, whoever you are in contact with.

AND NEVER BE ABUSIVE OR OFFENSIVE: Sometimes you find an instructor who tries to motivate you by putting you down, yelling or being sarcastic. They have missed the point. There is a big difference between motivating with intensity and being a jerk. Treat people like you want to be treated. Be kind, be spirited , be encouraging, be an example.

Students are encouraged to:
(1) memorize
(2) strive to understand
(3) live out the tenets of the Student Creed on a daily basis

This Creed, which could be called a Code, is designed to result in a Lifestyle. In 1970 the band Crosby, Stills, Nash, & Young released their hit album, DÉJÀ VU, which included the hit, **Teach Your Children**. The song was written by Graham Nash while he was with the group The Hollies, though The Hollies never recorded it. **Teach Your Children** was countrified by the leader, singer, guitarist for The Grateful Dead, Mr. Jerry Garcia. I like this song because it speaks of passing on to the next generation a Creed or a Code: *You who are on the road/ Must have a code that you can live by*.

In Wado Ryu karate, the things I learned in the dojo I intend to develop in an atmosphere of self-discipline, that will be manifested towards myself, to others, to my fellow human beings in a non-abusive and non-offensive manner. This attitude really does go along with what I have already learned in my walk as a Christian, as I follow the words and code and creed of Jesus. The Bible is my manufacturer's handbook (where my code and creed are found). If I live my life out loud, by following these principles, my world - the place where I come into contact with others - will be better off.

I love how my karate experience underscores my walk with the Lord.

CHAPTER KU (NINE)
HEAT IT AND BEAT IT

"The only time success comes before sweat - is in the dictionary."

- Unknown

That anonymous saying is painted on the wall of Bill Taylor's Bushido School of Karate on Broad Street in Murfreesboro, Tennessee. I would repeat that saying more than once on my journey to the black belt as sweat poured into my eyes, saturating my uniform and baptizing me in the suffering pool of a hard class.

I remember one particularly challenging class led by Mr. Taylor. As I was pushing it hard, over and over and over again, at one point he uttered the phrase, "Heat it and beat it!" The *heat* part referred to the continual motion of the techniques with its resultant sweat. Sometimes, the heat is turned up to enhance the dojo ambiance. The *beat* part was the stretching of ourselves beyond the point of what we thought we could do. Muscles getting tired, kicks not as high, punches to the point of weakness were all part of the beating.

Of course the analogy is sword-making; taking steel, heating it up to the point of being pliable and then at just the right time a hammer comes down on the melted metal and begins to form, shape, fashion the lump of metal into a finely honed weapon. The sword was conceived in the bellowed fires of the furnace and then birthed by the pounding of the hammer, its fine edge honed to razor sharpness by rubbing against flint rock.

Welcome to karate.

The black belt examination is broken down into four parts. One part is a community service project, because karate is more than kicking, it is helping our fellow man (see the chapter on the Student Creed). Another part of the examination is collecting our thoughts and writing a muse on *What it Means to Me to be a Black Belt* (see the introduction of this book). During the practical examination, where you are tested on what you have learned, you have many pairs of Black Belt eyes on you, walking around with clipboards, determining if you are worthy of the prize. At our school they add one more portion to the examination the day before the Federation Examination - the endurance test.

The endurance test is where they take the *heat it and beat it* concept, and ratchet it up about 20 notches. This is where black belt candidates are pushed to the limit and beyond. For an hour or more (the time can be more or less based on the spirit of the examinees), the candidate is in constant motion, going up and down the floor, throwing techniques, running kata and in general being pushed to the limit. The most helpful information that I received prior to this test was, "Don't give up. Keep moving."

I remember vividly going up and down the dojo floor, kicking a front kick (Mai Geri), over and over and over and over and over (talk about heating it), and over. My kicks started off high, but as we continued the kicks got lower and lower. If a leprechaun attacked me at that very moment, my kick may have been able to reach his ankle. At one point one of the instructors said as a word of encouragement, "We don't walk on my floor Mr. Boyd. Those are suppose to be kicks. Get them up."

I have found that every instructor at Bill Taylor's Bushido School of Karate brings something different to the table. I learn something at every class. I am stretched to a certain point. I am corrected and educated about something. Some instructors are gung ho. They believe if you are not sweating you are not working hard enough, so they are going to make you sweat. These classes are fast-paced and brutal. Other classes are more informative, and we practice kata and technique at a slower pace. The little known secret is this: you can workout with spirit, and sweat as much as if you were being pushed beyond your limits in another class. This goes back to the Student Creed with your intentions for self-discipline. You can also come to a class, mail in your workout and never break a sweat, .but the cause and effect of not *heating it and beating it* is like the difference between having a plastic sword and a real sword.

In my Christian walk, which is reflected by my walk in the *real world*, I need a little *heat and beat* so I can be a finely honed instrument of righteousness.

"Therefore let us be diligent to enter that rest, so that no one will fall, through following the same example of disobedience. For the Word of God is living and active and sharper than any two-edged sword, and piercing as far as the division of soul and spirit of both joints and marrow and able to judge the intentions of the heart."

Hebrews 4:11-12

You can't expect to have a finely honed sword in your spiritual life while allowing your Bible to sit on your coffee table, gathering dust. Part of the *heat and beat* process is reading the Word, studying the Word, praying the Word, applying the Word. The sweat process is doing this, even if you don't feel like it. Jesus said, *"If you abide in me and my Words abide in you, you can ask whatever you wish, and it shall be done unto you."* (John 15:7) The *heating and beating* is found in the abiding.

ABIDE: menō *(men'-o)*=A primary verb; to *stay* (in a given place, state, relation or expectancy): - abide, continue, dwell, endure, be present, remain, stand, tarry (for), X thine own.

The abiding is the continuation in the face of adversity to endure, to stand strong. How many of us have reached the limit of our endurance and at some point just gave up? It has been said to me and the class more than once, "The only way that you will not get your black belt, is if you quit coming."

Another aspect of this walk, this lifestyle, this process - is faith. We are told in Romans 1:17, *"For in it (the gospel), the righteousness of God is revealed from faith to faith, as it is written, But the righteous man shall live by faith."* (see also Habakkuk 2:4; Galatians 3:11; Hebrews 10:38)

"Now faith is the assurance (the confirmation, the title-deed) of the things [we] hope for, being the proof of things [we] do not see and the conviction of their reality - faith perceiving as real fact what is not revealed to the senses."

Hebrews 11:1

Without this thing called faith, we cannot please God.

"But without faith it is impossible to please and be satisfactory to Him. For whoever would come near to God must (necessarily) believe that God exists and that He is the Rewarder of those who earnestly and diligently seek Him (out)."

Hebrews 11:6

Notice that the key to this God-pleasing faith is earnest and diligent seeking, not just passively inquiring of Him. There is an aspect of *keeping on keeping on, heat and beat* seeking. The great debate throughout the ages has been - is the key just believing, having faith; or is it works, practiced continually that will bring us success?

In the book of James there is a call to not just believe something, but to let that belief work its way into your life. Energy and power are the keys to *heat and beat* in the same way that faith and works are the springboards of Christianity. What you *believe* is manifested in what you *do*. That principle is true in karate or Christianity. The action of heating and beating will manifest results, whether a spiritual walk or a black belt.

"So also faith if it does not have works (deeds and actions of obedience to back it up), by itself is destitute of power - inoperative, dead. But some one will say [to you then], You [say you] have faith and I have [good] works. Now you show me your [alleged] faith apart from any [good] works [if you can], and I by [good] works [of obedience] will show you my faith."

James 2:17-18

FAITH: Pistis (*pis'-tis*)= *persuasion*, that is, *credence*; moral *conviction* (of *religious* truth, or the truthfulness of God or a religious teacher), especially *reliance* upon Christ for salvation; abstractly *constancy* in such profession; by extension the system of religious (Gospel) *truth* itself: - assurance, belief, believe, faith, fidelity.

ENERGY/WORKS: Ergon (*er'-gon*)=From ἔργω ergō (a primary but obsolete word; to *work*); *toil* (as an effort or occupation); by implication an *act:* - deed, doing, labour, work.

POWER: Dunamis (*doo'-nam-is*)= *force* (literally or figuratively); specifically miraculous *power* (usually by implication a *miracle* itself): - ability, abundance, meaning, might (-ily, -y, -y deed), (worker of) miracle (-s), power, strength, violence, mighty (wonderful) work.

I like karate because it takes me from one point (white belt) to another point (black belt) and all points in between (yellow belt to brown belt). One thing that our school is *not* known for is being a so-called Belt Factory. Just because you show up for class does not mean that you are given a belt. Each time a belt is wrapped around your waist, you can be sure that you earned that belt by blood, sweat and tears. You went through the *heat and beat* process, and did not give up. You became, or are in the process of becoming, a sharp sword.

By the time you take your black belt exam you will have been through the examination/testing process at least 11 times. You will not be recommended to take your black belt exam, or any other exam for that matter, until you are ready. Time is a factor - but the other factor is you *not giving up* in the face of hardship. During my years of training I have seen people come and go, but those who are still by my side .have a sharpness developed, and character proven in their lives.

Relating my karate experiences in the dojo to my spiritual life, the Apostle Paul speaks of the process.

"Therefore we are justified - acquitted, declared righteous, and given a right standing with God - through faith, let us [grasp the fact that we] have [the peace of reconciliation] to hold and to enjoy, peace with God through our Lord Jesus Christ, the Messiah, the Anointed One. Through Him also we have [our] access (entrance, introduction) by faith into this grace - state of God's favor - in which we [firmly and safely] stand. And let us also be full of joy now! Let us exult and triumph in our troubles and rejoice in our sufferings, knowing that pressure and affliction and hardship produces patient and unswerving endurance. And endurance (fortitude) develops maturity of character - that is, approved faith and tried integrity. And character [of this sort] produces [the habit of] joyful and confident hope of eternal salvation. Such hope never

disappoints or deludes or shames us, for God's love has been poured out in our hearts through the Holy Spirit Who has been given to us."

Romans 5:1-5 (*AB*)

Life ain't easy. As you go through the process of pressure, affliction and hardship, you will develop proven character in your life. So it is with your karate journey. If you endure the *heating and beating* of the process of development, you will come out on the other side with the true, proven, martial arts character.

CHAPTER JU (TEN)
THE ART OF KIAI
Spirit Shout

As we go up and down the dojo floor, throwing kicks and punches, the count is on. With each move there is a count. Ichi, Ni, San, Chi, Go, Roku, Sichi, Hachi, Ku - and then the big number ten; JU!

When the number 10 - Ju - is counted, something is expected to happen. What should happen is what is known as a *Kiai!*

Back in the early 70s, when the karate craze was at its zenith, you could hear a Kiai on the radio, at the movies, in the back yard as kids were kicking and punching. Carl Douglas had the big hit, "Kung Fu Fighting." "Everybody was Kung Fu Fighting." *Kiai!* "The fists were fast as lightning." *Kiai!* Bruce Lee's definitive karate movie, "Enter the Dragon," had the soundtrack music written by Lalo Schiffren, the same person who composed the iconic music of the "Mission Impossible" franchise. As the oriental sounding music flowed, it was punctuated by, *Kiai!* The plethora of movies being produced in China was filled with boards slapping boards to give the sound to the punches and kicks, dialogue in English that did not match up to the movement of the mouths and, of course, various sound effects to exemplify the *Kiai!* Bruce Lee was famous for his guttural growls and cat-like sounds that culminated in the Kiai as he kicked and punch.

The sound of the Kiai is as different as there are people doing it. Children sound different; adults sound different. It ranges from a weak *uh*, to a deep down, from-the-gut earthquake of a sound. I have an app on my i-Phone for karate terminology. The definition of Kiai is, "spirit shout." I like that definition, because a true Kiai reflects spirit, attitude, the flow of intensity released.

In Wado katas there is not a Kiai, but sometimes someone will break out with a *spirit shout* - and then almost apologize. The instructors will usually say, "Never apologize for spirit." At tournaments the Kiai is uttered during the kata to underscore the intensity, and to get the attention of the judges. In class, sometimes as the count is fast approaching Ju (ten), someone will Kiai on Ni (nine). A little premature, but again, we should never apologize for spirit. Sometimes, when I am teaching a white belt class, I like to end by running the First Basic Kata with everyone giving a Kiai on every technique. The First Basic Kata has twenty moves, so that would be twenty Kiais. The room becomes energized, and that energy overflows into the gallery where parents and other people are sitting, and you can see the conversations stop, heads look up and smiles come on their faces. Spirit is contagious! The spirit shout should not only scare whoever is attacking you, but should also energize your performance. On a practical side, taking air and forcing it out is also a good way to tighten up the stomach muscles to help absorb a kick.

The spiritual version of the Kiai (Spirit Shout) is the word Praise. In some corners of the Christian faith quietness is considered to be the ultimate in spiritual reverence. But quietness is only one aspect of reverence. The ancient Hebrew word, *Halal*, translated as *Praise*, reflects the rowdy nature of worship.

PRAISE: hālal (*haw-lal'*)=A primitive root; to be clear (originally of sound, but usually of color); to shine hence to make a show to boast and thus to *be* clamorously foolish to *rave,* causatively to celebrate.

This is where we get the word *hallelujah*, which means *praise to God* (Jahweh). One place this word appears is in Psalm 150, and here it reflects a spirited, rowdy worship of God. Think about the various reflections of the definition:

(1) Be clear
(2) To shine
(3) To make a show
(4) To boast
(5) To be clamorously foolish
(6) To rave
(7) To celebrate

For me, the word *praise* (halal), is my spirit shout, my Kiai to the Lord.

Praise (hallal) the Lord
Praise (hallal) God in His sanctuary
Praise (hallal) in His mighty expanse
Praise (hallal) Him for His mighty deeds
Praise (hallal) Him according to His excellent greatness
Praise (hallal) Him with trumpet sound
Praise (hallal) Him with timbrel and dancing
Praise (hallal) Him with stringed instruments and pipe
Praise (hallal) with loud cymbals
Praise (hallal) with resounding cymbals
Let everything that has breath praise (hallal) the Lord
Praise (hallal) the Lord!

Psalm 150

I am trained as a Speech-Language Pathologist; one who studies the intricacies of sound production. Sound starts from a thought; what we want to express verbally. We breathe in air, and as we breathe out our vocal folds are set into motion. The vibratory sound that travels through our resonating cavities (throat, mouth, nose, etc.) is formed, and as we move our lips and tongue (the articulators), we vocalize what we want to express. A true Kiai is not *just* sound, but an expression of thought and desire manifested on our lips.

> The question is,
> "Are you breathing?"
>
> -Wayne Berry
> Worship Pastor,
> friend
> and musicologist

I believe that as the entire karate class comes together with a collective Kiai, we become One. We become a group of individuals on a journey, giving out a spirit shout. It is like we are giving a collective, '*Amen.*' In a church service, as the preacher is preaching his best, giving it all he has got, a non-responsive congregation can change the atmosphere of the church hall. That struggling preacher might call out, "Can I get an amen?" When I am teaching The Ruminator Sunday School Class, if nobody responds to my words, I'll say, "Somebody throw a dog a bone." I am looking for affirmation that what I am saying is true, that it means something, that I'm hitting home. Just as an *amen* will carry a struggling preacher along, so it is with a Kiai. The Kiai will rev you up if you are dragging in class.

AMEN: Hebrew: 'âmên (*aw-mane'*) sure; abstractly *faithfulness*; adverbially *truly:* - Amen, so be it, truth. 'âman (*aw-man'*)=A primitive root; properly to *build up* or *support*; to *foster* as a parent or nurse; figuratively to *render* (or *be*) *firm* or faithful, to *trust* or believe, to be *permanent* or quiet; morally to *be true* or certain; once (in Isa 30:21) to *go to the right hand:* - hence assurance, believe, bring up, establish, + fail, be faithful (of long continuance, steadfast, sure, surely, trusty, verified), nurse, (-ing father), (put), trust, turn to the right.

AMEN: Greek: amēn (*am-ane'*)=Of Hebrew origin; properly *firm*, that is, (figuratively) *trustworthy*; adverbially *surely* (often as interjection *so be it*): - amen, verily.

The Kiai is an affirmation, an outward manifestation, of an inward desire. It is a declaration of what we believe and desire. It is the ultimate pep talk to ourselves and an agreement with our instructors and fellow students that we believe in what we are learning mentally and what we are expressing physically on the dojo floor. The Kiai is the internal *Yes!* expressed for all the world to know. We take no shame in gathering together with thousands of sports fans at a football game, a soccer game, a hockey game or at a concert of the latest flavor of musical tastes and cheer. We *throw down* unashamedly at these events. We *Halal*. We choose to: Praise; to be Clear (originally of sound, but usually of color); to Shine (to make a show); to Boast; to be Clamorously Foolish; to Rave; to Celebrate! Why not do the same on and off the dojo floor - in karate, in life, in church, where ever we are breathing.

The Kiai can become the reflection of our inward alive kata. A dead kata Kiai will dribble out over our lips, but an alive kata Kiai is a spirited shout to the world.

I discovered the idea of the word, *Yes,* as expressing affirmation, when I went to Kenya Africa as a teacher at a Youth With A Mission Discipleship Training School (YWAM DTS). It was an eclectic gathering of students, led by a man named John, from Tanzania. He was encouraging the students about the Lord meeting their financial needs.

"And my God will supply all your needs according to His riches in glory in Christ Jesus."

Philippians 4:19

John asked the student, "Do you believe that God will meet your needs according to His riches in glory in Christ Jesus?" There was a weak, *"Yes,"* voiced by the students. It was kind of like a weak Kiai at the count of Ju.

"You don't sound like you believe," John shot back. He repeated the question, but this time, on cue, everybody stretched out their right hands like they were cocking a rifle, and together as one unit pulled back their cocked fists and gave a collective, *"Yeesss!"*

The room reverberated with Yes, Amen, Hallal, *Kiai!*

The lesson I learned in the dojo - don't hold back; verbalize my internal Spirit Shout.

CHAPTER JU ICHI ICHI (ELEVEN)
SURPRISE, SURPRISE, SURPRISE

As the years pass you can get into what is known as a rut. A rut has been humorously defined as a grave with both ends knocked out. When we do the same thing over and over again, we risk losing focus. It's easy to just mindlessly go through the ritual of the mundane. This can include kata, our spiritual lives and our everyday, nitty gritty existence. As we walk out this sometimes mind-numbing existence, occasionally we are caught by surprise. This surprise can be a good thing or a bad thing, but whether it is good, bad or ugly, how you deal with the surprises in life will determine your future outcome.

On his project, *Charity of the Night*, singer/songwriter Bruce Cockburn speaks of this unexpected surprise. A couple of verses of his song, "The Whole Night Sky," speak loudly to me, because I have found myself there throughout my life.

Sometimes a wind comes out of nowhere, And knocks you off your feet/ And look, see my tears, They fill the whole night sky.

Or in the words of erstwhile purveyor of perpetual good humor, Gomer Pyle, "Surprise, surprise, surprise."

The wind that comes out of nowhere, speaks of things out of your control. I have literally been knocked off my feet. There were tears, internal and external. My train was derailed and I did feel desperate. The final line of that verse, *hanging from this highwire by the tatters of my faith*, really speaks to me of hanging onto what I believe by faith and not by sight. Let's look at some of the surprises that have come my way in my journey to black belt as I learn some lessons in the dojo.

FLYING PANTIES

I started back in karate in 2001. I got into my Gi (uniform) over at the Broad Street school. I was a lowly white belt and the locker room was packed, (It was easy to pack that locker room, because it was small, almost as if it was an actual locker) with 15 to 20 guys who were all trying to get dressed. Black Belts flowed through a sea of other colored belts. As I pulled out my uniform, which my lovely wife Brenda had washed for me, I gave a nice sharp flip of the uniform and prepared to stick my leg into the pants. Sudden something unexpected happened. A pair of my wife's panties came floating out of the pants leg. In a Matrix-like slow motion they seemed to hover in the air in suspended animation, then they slowly drifted to the floor. It seemed like every eye was on the floating panties, and then on me.

"Those panties aren't mine," I declared, loudly. "They belong to my wife."

Surprise, surprise, surprise!

After the laughter died down, I put on my uniform, tied my white belt around my waist and went out and practiced the *manly art of self defense.*

TIPTOE IN THE DOJO FLOOR

I am not the most graceful being on two feet. When Brenda and I were dating, we went to a lot of school dances, even though my dancing skills resembled a caveman shuffling back and forth.

In karate class one night while we were sitting in a circle, Mr. Holt called students to the center of the circle to perform whatever kata we were learning at the time. Eventually he called on me to perform Pinan Nidan. Now, my uniform was too long for me, and I had not had a chance to get it altered, so the pant legs were turned up into cuffs so they would not drag the ground. All eyes were focused on me as I hopped up, but when I began to step out my right big toe caught on cuff of my left pant leg and I went falling forward. At the time I weighted a lot (at one point over 320 pounds), and the principle of mass moving forward was in full vigor. I tumbled over, landed on my shoulder, rolled into the circle, and then rolled into an upright position, just as if I had planned it). Nervous laughter accompanied some *ooohs* and *aaahs*, and various people asked if I was all right. Surprise, surprise, surprise.

BREAKING CONCRETE BLOCK WITH MY HEAD

This event took place off of the dojo floor, during my other life as a Speech-Language Pathologist. I was at a patient's house, finishing up my visit. It was my last stop before going home for the day. As it was in the late fall, it was already dark outside. To get to my car I had to go down a flight of wooden stairs leading to the basement garage, which was poorly illuminated by a low-wattage bulb. There were at least 25 steps down into that dismal abyss. In one arm I carried my pack of equipment and tests, and under my other arm was my clipboard. Everything was going fine - until I reached the bottom step. I looked down at what I thought was the last step before the concrete garage floor. Surprise, surprise, surprise! There were actually two more steps. I stepped out expecting to touch my feet on the floor and instead encountered empty space. I went hurtling face-forward into the concrete block walls.

My glasses broke, blood splattered everywhere, both of my shoulders were in pain and I just laid there in a heap of startled surprise. It happened so quickly I could only lay there and wonder what had just occurred. The realization that I had fallen and hurt myself finally dawned on me. I got up and climbed back up those same steps and let the patient know what had happed. We stopped the bleeding, then I walked (much more carefully) down the steps again and got in my car. The pain in my shoulders was so intense I could not even lift my arms. I called Brenda, then drove myself all the way from from Hermitage, Tennessee to Stonecrest Hospital in Smyrna, Tennessee. I just wanted to get as close to home as possible.

They gave me drugs to help ease the pain - and I waited. A nurse asked me what I happened. I remember asking her if instead of putting down that I fell on the bottom steps of a parking garage, could she put down that I was fighting in a caged match and that although I looked like I lost, I had actually won. She said, 'No.' Surprise, surprise, surprise.

HERE TODAY - GONE TOMORROW

Years ago, early in my career as a Speech-Language Pathologist, I left my first job at Nashville Rehabilitation Hospital and went to work for a home health agency where I did Speech Therapy at hospitals, in homes and for the prison system. I had worked there for more than a year, and everything seemed to be going smoothly. The agency had always held weekly meetings, but on one particular week things were different. There were the mixture of our bosses, various therapists, office workers and three or four people we had never seen before. They informed us that in one month the business was shutting down. Totally. Surprise, surprise, surprise.

One minute I was gainfully employed and the next instant I was out of a job. The reaction in the room ranged from shocked silence, to soft crying, to overt cursing. Some of the employees had just been hired, and this was their first office meeting. There was the proverbial weeping and gnashing of teeth, and the bitterness in the room was palpable. I called my lovely wife Brenda and informed her that I no longer had a job. Her first reaction was literally, "Well, praise God. I wonder what He has for us next?"

The *next* was that I shifted to working for a hospital that I had been doing contract work for via the now defunct company. And I worked there for the next 15 years.

Surprises may start out negative, but they don't have to stay that way. I have found that when something bad happens, I can stand on the Word of God.

"For we know that all things (good, bad and ugly) can work together for good, to them that love the Lord and are called according to His purpose."

Romans 8:25

PRE-BLACK BELT SURPRISE

I was on the verge of taking my black belt examination. My belt was hanged on the wall with my name above it, the culmination of my years of training. All my hard work was about to pay off. This was not the time to ease off on my training; was time to crank it up a notch. I went to classes three times a week, increased my cardio workout and gave it everything I had. My body didn't always want to cooperate. Over the years I had injured my shoulders and knees on various occasions, and the fact is - I was getting older, and my body did not snap back quite as fast as it did in my younger days. But I persevered.

A couple of weeks before the examination, we were doing a drill where one student held the kicking shield as the other partner kicked. My partner failed to kick the center of the shield. His kick glanced of the edge of the shield and caught me at the knee, and my knee was already hurting. A few days later, I trained alone with my instructor, performing alternate roundhouse kicks on the Wavemaster. I was pumped and kicked with all of my strength, but I could feel something wasn't right in my left knee.

The week before my examination (the endurance and Federation), I was in a large class of at least 30 students, many of whom had already earned their black belts. Our instructor called me to the center to run various katas. It was almost a rite of passage for those transitioning from brown belt to black belt, and I was pumped. I wanted to give it everything I had.

The instructor called out, "Pinan Nidan."

I felt like I could conquer the world. I went into my first move with the otoshi (dropping movement) of the hammer fist in my side-viewing cat stance. I flowed into a moving forward front punch with power, then turned into the next moves. I was invincible. I moved down the floor, intending to perform three high blocks. I moved with such intensity on the first block that I heard what sounded like my uniform ripping.

Only it was not my uniform. It was my rotator cuff.

As soon as I heard the rip, I experienced intense pain and my right arm fell to my side. I could not lift it up. I was in agony. Surprise, surprise, surprise.

I finished the kata, using my left hand to lift my right hand. Days before I was to take the most important examination of my karate career, and I was popping ibuprofen and alternating hot and cold compresses on my shoulder and left knee. I managed to make it through the endurance exam, but on the day of the Federation exam, I was in severe pain and limping on my left knee. I would not be denied my moment. When Mr. Taylor asked me how I was doing, I told him honestly that my knee was hurt and that I was limping some.

"Don't let them see you limp," he advised.

Those words gave me the courage to accomplish my task. I prayed for strength, and God gave it. I received my black belt.

The following Monday I was still limping. I had an MRI, and ended up having surgery on my left knee.

LIFE SURPRISES

I have found that life does not always pan out the way that you plan it out. As we walk out our lives in this land that I like to call, The Land of Nitty Gritty, stuff happens. I have also found out, on the dojo floor and in my Manufacturer's Handbook (the Bible), that how we react or respond will make all the difference in our journey. You already know that all things (the good, the bad and the ugly) can work together for our good because we (1) love the Lord, and (2) are called according to His purpose.

In Genesis, we see the story of Joseph, who had a dream. His jealous brothers faked his death, threw him into a pit and then sold him into slavery. Boy, talk about a dysfunctional family. Joseph experienced one surprise after another. He was elevated to a position of power and at last came face to face with his brothers - the same brothers who sold him in to slavery. They were fearful for their lives (and well they should have been; Joseph held the power of life and death), but instead of condemnation, he uttered these words:

"Do not be afraid, for am I in God's place? As for you, you meant evil against me/you meant it for harm. But God meant it for good in order to bring about this present result, to preserve many people alive."

Genesis 50:19-20

GODISNOWHERE

When people look at the letters, GODISNOWHERE, they may see different things. Depending on their circumstances, they may see:

(1) good
(2) bad
(3) ugly

They will either react in the negative or respond in the positive. Here are three options on how to view this phrase.

- GODISNOWHERE: God is NO where.
- GODISNOWHERE: God is NOW here.
- GODISNOWHERE: God I SNOW here.

How you look at it determines what you do. When life throws me a *Surprise, Surprise, Surprise!* Moment, I can either act as if *God is now here* - and in control - or I can go the negative route and act as if I am all alone with no hope. The *snow* one is optional.

CHAPTER JU ICHI NI (TWELVE)
MOKUSOU MEDITATION MOMENT

"Ohooooooooooooooommmmmmmmmmmmmmmmmmm"

- Sound associated with *meditation*

Most people's concept of meditation is twisting your body into a pretzel-like pattern, holding your fingers in a circular fashion with your fingertips and your thumb together, emptying your mind of all thought, embracing total nothingness while allowing your mind to be filled with some kind of demonic influence and then uttering mindlessly over and over a sound or word in the form of a mantra until you reach some state if nirvana. This thing called *meditation* is perceived to be some mystical moment that transcends the physical.

In the 60s, Transcendental Meditation was all the rage. I never could figure out what it had to do with teeth (transcend-DENTAL? What is that? A method to deal with the pain as the dentist is drilling on your teeth?) While there may be those transcendent moments for some people in the martial arts community, in all of my years of practicing the martial arts I have never been required to, or encouraged to, transcend my mind to increase my physical being in performing my art. My kicks have never got any higher because of mind games. Physical stretching and daily practice is what gets your kicks higher, which may explain why my kicks are not higher than they are or should be.

I do know that when we come to an attention stance (Musubi Dachi) in preparation to Rei (bow), we are encouraged to take the quiet moment to clear our minds of everything that would distract us for the next 50 minutes. Leave your worries and cares outside of the dojo doors and focus on learning and practicing the way of harmony and peace (Wado Ryu). The worries and cares of the world that we live in will suck the life and energy out of our physical bodies. Anything that distracts us and commands our attention opens the door for someone's foot to come flying out of nowhere and smack us in the head.

Once, when sparring with Mr. Wilson, I was distracted by a punch and his foot came up, seemingly out of nowhere, and smacked me in the head. Oh, it was a controlled kick. He focused and held back the full power of the kick. But it got my attention. Part of the kick hit me in the eye, and I wanted to pause to nurse my wounded body and pride. I will never forget these words of wisdom from Mr. Wilson, "Don't stop, because I'm not."

I have meditated on those words of wisdom often, and the cause and effect of that meditation is this: If you're sparring in class, keep your hands up and don't stop.

This thing call Mukuso, meditation, does not end after you bow into class. The thought process should carry over into the learning and practice process. When you make mistakes, forget moves, get hit - don't you think that focus and awareness brought on by Mukuso would be beneficial to help you rise above the distractions? I think so. Now don't get me wrong. I am writing about a standard that I wish and hope and strive for, but I don't always do it.

This thing called meditation is not limited to the dojo floor. Remember the subtitle of this book is, *Lessons I Learned in the*

Dojo. Don't you think this concept of taking a moment to empty our minds of all the worries, fears, doubt, unbelief, anxiety and tension that tends to overwhelm us as we step out on to the floor of our lives would be a good thing? When the surprises of life smack us in the head, wouldn't it be nice if we remain focused and not quite so distracted as the barrage continues? Wouldn't it be nice if we could focus on the tasks at hand?

If you have not figured it out by now, the lessons I learned in the dojo, I had already learned in my walk as a believer and follower of Jesus Christ. The lessons are underscored and validated by the Word of God, which I like to refer to as The Manufacturer's Handbook, aka The Bible.

For the past 20-something years, I have taught a Sunday School Class called The Ruminators Sunday School Class. There was a point in my Christian journey where I was sick and tired of Christians and Christianity in general (but that's another story). I found myself licking my wounds at a church called Smyrna Assembly of God (now named Springhouse Worship and Arts Center). I had previously taught Sunday School, but I vowed *never* (never say never) to teach it again. Through a series of events, and encouragement from a guy named Mark Robertson, I dipped my toes back into the teaching pool. I taught a class on The Topical Memory System, by a group called The Navigators. The premise for the class was that we would memorize 60 Scripture verses while studying the surrounding context. I've said all of that to say this - one of the verses changed my life.

"This book of the Law (the Word) shall not depart from your mouth, but you shall meditate on it (the Law/Word) day and night so that you may be careful to do according to all that is written in it, for then you will make your way prosperous, and then you will have good success."

Joshua 1:8

Wow, meditation has a direct impact on prosperity and success - and not just success, but *good* success.

MEDITATION: hâgâh *(baw-gaw')*=A primitive root; to *murmur* (in pleasure or anger); by implication to *ponder:* - imagine, meditate, mourn, mutter, roar, X sore, speak, study, talk, utter. hâgîyg *(baw-gheeg')*=From an unused root akin to; properly a *murmur*, that is, *complaint:* - meditation, musing. hâgâh *(baw-gaw')*= to *murmur* (in pleasure or anger); by implication to *ponder:* - imagine, meditate, mourn, mutter, roar, X sore, speak, study, talk, utter.

RUMINATE: Verb (used without object)

(1) to chew the cud, as a ruminant.
(2) to meditate or muse; ponder.

RUMINANT: Noun

(1) any even-toed, hoofed mammal of the suborder Ruminantia, being comprised of cloven-hoofed, cud-chewing quadrupeds, and including, besides domestic cattle, bison, buffalo, deer, antelopes, giraffes, camels and chevrotains.
(2) ruminating; chewing the cud.
(3) contemplative; meditative: a ruminant scholar.
(4) any artiodactyl mammal of the suborder *Ruminantia* , the members of which chew the cud and have a stomach of four compartments, one of which is the rumen. The group includes deer, antelopes, cattle, sheep and goats
(5) any other animal that chews the cud, such as a camel
(6) of, relating to, or belonging to the suborder *Ruminantia*
(7) of members of this suborder and related animals, such as camels
(8) chewing the cud; ruminating
(9) meditating or contemplating in a slow quiet way

Now, I know that this may be more information than you want to know about rumination, but it is key for me about this thing we call meditation, and it's all about the *cud*.

As the ruminant eats food (whether it be oats or grass), it chews, masticates, and then swallows. A ruminant has four chambers of the stomach (one being the rumen). The swallowed food journeys down through the four chambers of the stomach, and then regurgitates it back up in the form of a CUD. When you see a cow out in the field chewing the cud, the cow has a meditative look on its face. This is where my Sunday School class got its name, from the book of Joshua, chapter one, verse 8. We chew on the Word of God, like a cow chews the cud. We meditate, we haw-gaw (Hebrew), we ruminate (Latin) the Word of God.

I like the way God has a sense of humor; or at the least irony.

(1) This Book of the Law (The Word of God)
(2) Shall not depart from your mouth (the place of speaking and chewing)
(3) But you shall meditate (ruminate, mutter under your breath, in your mouth)
(4) So that you may be careful to do (action springing from meditation)
(5) All that is written in it (the Word, or the cud)
(6) For then (cause and effect coming into play)
(7) You (not anyone else, but you)
(8) Will make your way (faith put into action)
(9) Prosperous (enough to meet your need and an overflow to help others)
(10) And then you will have Good Success (accomplishing the purposes of God in your life)

This meditation process in every area of life - whether it be in the dojo, in everyday life, in Christianity - is more than just emptying the mind of the negative, but filling it with the positive. I fill my mind, begin to ruminate and then do what needs to be done. I think about a technique and do the technique. I do that all the time as I work out. I think or mutter under my breath my next move (it really does help) and at some point it turns into an automatic response. So it is with the way I conduct my life and the way I conduct my Christianity. It becomes natural and not forced.

"Finally brethren, whatever is true, whatever is honorable, whatever is right, whatever is pure, whatever is lovely, whatever is of a good report, if there is any excellence, and if anything worthy of praise, allow your mind to dwell (think on) these things."

Philippians 4:8

"For the rest, brethren, whatever is true, whatever is worthy of reverence and is honorable and seemly, whatever is just, whatever is pure, whatever is lovely and lovable, whatever is kind and winsome and gracious, if there is any virtue and excellence, if there is anything worthy of praise, think on and weigh and take account of these things - fix your minds on them."

Philippians 4:8 (AB)

We as human beings, as people who call ourselves Christians, as people who practice the martial arts, need to remember that people are watching us. We need to step up to the plate and be examples to others. The verse that follows Philippians 4:8 - that would be Verse 9 - encourages others to practice the way that we let/allow our minds to dwell/meditate on good things.

"The things that you have learned and received and heard and seen in me, practice these things and the God of peace will be with you."

Philippians 4:9

Over these past few years I have learned, received, heard and seen these thing in others at the dojo. Now, I take them out into my world and begin to practice them.

CHAPTER JU ICHI SAN (Thirteen)
THE ZEN OF ZANSHIN

"I keep my eyes wide open all the time."
"I Walk The Line," by Johnny Cash

To start off this chapter on the Zen of Zanshin, I would like to quote the Bruce Lee of country music - Johnny Cash - "I keep my eyes wide open all the time."

The Zen of Zanshin is really the Art of Awareness. Zanshin is simply the awareness of your surroundings. If people would just become more aware of their surroundings it could lead to a decrease in muggings, kidnappings, fender-benders, blind-sidings and multiple other surprising moments in our lives. So many times we go through this world with a happy-go-lucky, not-a-care-in-the-world attitude, and we are oblivious to what is going on around us. Then, when something unexpected happens, we smack our foreheads and say, "Wow, I didn't see that coming."

Sometimes we are so close to our situation, that our vision, our insights, our judgments may be clouded by the familiar. It would help to have an eye in the back of our heads, but since that is not possible we need to develop the Zen of Zanshin. That's right. I said *develop*. This development is a progressive practice of heightening our awareness of our surroundings.

The surroundings in our lives are in flux, a constant state of change, as we weave in and out of circumstances, situations and places throughout our days and nights. What must remain constant are our levels of awareness - and even they change from one level to another depending upon the moment of the time-space continuum. The often quoted maxim on change is: "the only thing that is constant is change." There are various changes in that quote on change, but the original is acknowledge as coming from Heraclitus of Ephesus, a Greek philosopher who was known for his thoughts on the doctrine of change, which was, according to him, "central to the universe." Many have quoted old Heraclitus, from politicians to rock stars. Here are some variations on his quote.

"There is nothing permanent except change."
"Nothing is permanent except change."
"The only constant is change"
"Change is the only constant"
"Change alone is unchanging."

If things are in this state of constant flux, and circumstances, situations, people and events are ever changing, then we might consider taking Bruce Lee's advice:

"Empty your mind, be formless, shapeless - like water. Now you put water into a cup, it become the cup, you put water into a bottle, it becomes the bottle, you put it in a teapot, it becomes the teapot. Now water can flow or it can crash. Be water, my friend."

Bruce Lee

I like that last sentence. It reminds me of a current beer commercial on T.V. where the adventuresome man encourages us to, "Stay thirsty, my friends." Bruce ends with, "Be water, my friend." What Bruce is encouraging us to do is to be adaptable to every situation. It is like Sensai Taylor states, "Fighting is a game of adjustments." Another great piece of advice is; "If you find you are digging yourself into a hole - stop digging."

We do these self-adjustments all of the time. When you walk down the street and see your reflection in a shop window, if you notice your hair is out of place, you instinctively reach up and make an adjustment, by combing it. Or if your fly is unzipped, you adjust by zipping up. You've become aware of your appearance and you adjust accordingly. That may seem silly, but that is Zanshin in the mundane and trivial. How much more important is it to expand our awareness and make adjustments in other areas of our lives.

On September 1, 2001 (9/11) the United States was attacked by terrorists who flew two airliners into the Twin Towers in New York City. No one suspected. No one saw it coming. Our guard was down, and right before our very eyes those two magnificent towers crumbled to the ground, killing thousands including the 19 terrorists involved.

After the attack, the awareness level in this country went up greatly. A safety alert code was developed based on colors representing the perceived potential of terror risk. More than a decade later, we are still on alert. Every time we go to the airport to board a flight, security is high. Some believe these precautions have gone overboard, and I don't disagree, particularly when I'm inconvenienced by increasingly invasive security scans at various checkpoints, but the idea of being aware, alert and ready is still on everyone's mind.

Will McFarland, who was one of the session players in the famous Muscle Shoals recording community released an album that I am listening to as I pound the keys to this book. The project is called "Ax to the Roots." It's a guitar-driven, bluesy collection of songs. He is taking his ax (guitar) and laying it to the roots of things that keep us from growing in the Kingdom. His song called "Be There in that Number" came up, and it sure hits the spot of what we are talking about. Zanshin. Awareness. Eyes open. Here are some of the lyrics:

BE THERE IN THAT NUMBER

I got my eyes wide open
I'm looking around
I'm paying attention
To what's coming down
It's on the horizon
It's in the air
Marching in. I want to be there

Of course, this song is a play on the old hymn, "When the Saints Come Marching In," which is about the coming of the Lord and how we are admonished to keep our eyes wide open, looking, expecting the return of the Lord.

Just as our government has developed a color-coded threat level to help us understand the perceived danger of a terrorist attack, at our dojo we have been given color codes to keep in mind when we are walking in this world that we live in. These color codes could save our lives if, or when, we are attacked. I have taken the root of this color code system and personalized it for me.

WHITE: This is when there is no threat of danger, when we can let our guard down. It is the place where we feel comfortable. When I am in the confines of my home, eating dinner, watching T.V., talking to Brenda or Phillip I do not feel threatened. (Note: Not everyone has a safe, secure home environment. Your home might have a higher risk for domestic violence, which you must be on alert for. Threat levels can change quickly, even in environments you usually think of as being completely safe.)

YELLOW: This is elevated to a cautionary status. When I am walking in unknown territories, in new situations, going outside to get into my car at night from a store, my senses are heightened. I begin to look around, scan the area, observe for the unusual. Nothing is happening. No one is attacking. But I am more *aware* of my surroundings. When passing by a dark alley I look in the shadows, behind the bushes, etc. When I visit a patient's house doing speech therapy, my Yellow Awareness goes up to compensate for potential problems. For example, I might have a patient with psychiatric problems. If the patient's home is configured in such a way that I would be sitting in a corner, away from a door, I will rearrange my seating arrangements so I am not blocked in and no one can sneak up behind me. There is no imminent threat, only an increase potential. I am therefore more aware of my surroundings and take control *before* anything could possibly happen.

As I walk to get into my car, my eyes scan the parking lot, my keys are in my hand ready to unlock my car door, and my keys are placed strategically in my hands to use as a weapon if need be. Even though there is no immediate danger, my safety radar is up.

RED: The threat level rises to Red when my cautionary awareness has spotted danger; someone coming my way, someone mouthing off, someone stepping out of the shadows and following me. This puts me on high alert. Although nothing has happened yet, to my mind, danger is at hand. My karate skills are in ready stance (heiko dachi). I am ready for anything that may transpire. I can adjust my pathway, retreat into a place of safety, alert others around me of the impending danger, but I am definitely ready for attack.

BLACK: The attack is on. This is no time to formulate a plan. This is no time to begin to learning karate. This is no time to hesitate, because if you hesitate you die. Whatever happens, *don't go with anyone, anywhere*. They might tell you that if you don't go with them they will kill you. Let them try. You have more chance of dying if they can get you away to a private place. Once the attack is on, fight! Resist, make noise, kick, punch, bite. You are no longer *at risk* - you are fighting for you life. Of course, if someone approaches you with a weapon and demands your wallet or purse, give it to them. Remember, the strategy is to stay alive. But once the altercation becomes physical, don't just stand there and let them abuse, and possibly even kill you. You might as well .go out with a fight.

It is at this time that the wisdom of Sensei Taylor rings true. "Fighting is a game of adjustments." So are alertness levels. They can change in a moment, and you have to be willing and ready to change also or you will be stuck on one level when you should have adjusted and be fighting on a different level.

These color coded levels were designed for physical attacks, but they can be applied to any area of your life; at home, at work. in your relationships. For example, if you are home with your wife and all is

> "Fighting is a game of adjustments."
>
> Sensei Bill Taylor

well, the White level is intact. But what if you notice that your wife is not talking, or is sighing, or is huffing and puffing. Code Yellow - something is up. You try to quiz her about what's wrong. She says "Nothing," but there is an intense look in your direction, or a quiver in her voice, or a slight tear in her eyes. Code Red - danger is imminent. And before you know it, *Bam!* An all out war has broken out in the squared circle of you home. You're personal environment is at Code Black! The key to handling this kind of situation is to diffuse with love, understanding and forgiveness, and to yield your right to be right.

The Bible offers some sound advice on diffusing situations and going from Code Red or Black back down to Code White.

"Be angry, and yet do not sin, do not let/allow the sun to go down on your anger, and do not give the devil an opportunity."

Ephesians 4:26-27

The key is to have your Zanshin radar operating, and nip the little things in the bud before they escalate to Code Black.

CHAPTER JU ICHI CHI (Fourteen)
MORE POWER TO YA

"Power to the people!
Power to the people!
Power to the people!
Power to the people!
Right on!"

"Power To The People"
by John Lennon and the Plastic Ono Band

"Power to the peep hole!
Power to the peep hole!"

"Luther The Anthropoid (Ape Man)"
by Jimmy Caster and the Caster Bunch

"Today we learned in agony of war that great power involves great
responsibility."

Franklin Delano Roosevelt, 1945

"With great power comes great responsibility."

Peter Parker's (Spider-Man) Uncle Ben

"...and from everyone who has been given much shall much be required
and to whom they entrusted much, of him they will ask all the more."

Jesus, Luke 12:38

Power in karate is key to technique, but the way that you deliver that power is what will determine the outcome of your technique. In Wado Ryu, power is not hitting as hard as you can. The nature of power in our style of karate can be deceptive. In the natural you would think that the bigger the man, the more powerful the man, and there is some truth in that. But in the dojo a man's bulk is not what will determine the power in his kicks and punches. I have seen many larger people who have weak kicks. Their power is diffused by their attempts to bully their way through a fight, while the smaller, smarter opponent has learned the secrets of power. Their power is not based on brute force.

I have watch videos of Bruce Lee giving demonstrations of his one inch punch at karate tournaments in California. Bruce would stand with his fist one inch away from a victim, I mean a helper, and with one punch from one inch away, the helper is sent sprawling back into a chair and the chair is turned over. Bruce Lee was a small man. A well-developed small man, but small man none the less. When you watch that punch in slow motion, you see a key to the power. There is a twist of the body, .a shifting of weight that generates into the hand, then into the target. The source of power is not limited to just one thing, but multiple things that when working together form a synergistic increase in the ability to generate power.

Oh, to be sure, kicking and punching hard is a factor in the task at hand, but it is not the only factor. During an examination at the school, Sensai Taylor had one of the students to demonstrate a technique. After the girl performed the tasks, Sensai Taylor made sure to point out that she was making her uniform sleeve snap with the punch, because she was punching with power. In class, in examinations and in life in general, when you kick, punch or just live life with power, there is a snap to it.

The formula for power in karate is body weight + movement = momentum. When you take that formula, then focus the punch, you have got power. In Mr. Taylor's book "Wado Ryu: a Fighter's Perspective," he states, "Power in junzuki (moving forward front punch) is generated by funneling your body weight into the punch."

Another aspect of power generation is: when throwing a punch, as the punch goes forward, at the end of the punch, when you make contact with the target, twist the hand and then recoil the fist back. The snap of the punch and the twist of the hand, is like the crack of a bullwhip that goes out, reaches the target and then is snapped by pulling it back. I have found (as revealed by my teachers over and over again), that power comes from the hips. The subtle twisting of the hips is a dynamic power generator.

One punch that demonstrates this thing called power is the Gyakusuki (reverse punch). With the Ouizuki (front jab) it goes out and sets up the power punch. Oh don't get me wrong, the Ouizuki can hurt, but it is not as powerful (full of power) as the reverse punch. What sets the reverse punch apart from the front jab is the combination of twisting, momentum and waving/leaning of the upper body. As I tell the students that I teach, "There's power in da hips."

With the Gyakuzuki, you can demonstrate the hip turn by watching the belt. As you initiate the punch, the reverse arm (opposite of the foot that is out front), you come up on the toes of the back foot and twist the heel outward and twist the hips. You should physically see your belt turning and swinging with the hips. I will have the students stand around the Wavemaster (a bag for kicking and punching) and have them throw the Gyakuzuki without the toe and heel action. Two things are evident; no power, and less reach. But when you implement the toe and heel action, which in turn sets in motion the hips and the belt swaying into the turning of the hips, you extend your reach and the punch is much harder as it combines with the twisting of the fist and lands on the designated target. *Power generated!* The students not only see it, they feel it. Combine this with a powerful Kiai and you have the synergistic quality of power.

In the Greek language there are multiple words for the English word, power. Here are a few of these words and we will see how they apply to our lives.

POWER/AUTHORITY: Exousia *(ex-oo-see'-ah)*= (in the sense of *ability*); *privilege*, that is, (subjectively) *force, capacity, competency, freedom*, or (objectively) *mastery* (concretely *magistrate, superhuman, potentate, token of control*), delegated *influence:* - authority, jurisdiction, liberty, power, right, strength.

POWER: Dunamis *(doo'-nam-is)*= *force* (literally or figuratively); specifically miraculous *power* (usually by implication a *miracle* itself): - ability, abundance, meaning, might (-ily, -y, -y deed), (worker of) miracle (-s), power, strength, violence, mighty (wonderful) work. dunamai *(doo'-nam-ahee)*=Of uncertain affinity; to *be able* or *possible:* - be able, can (do, + -not), could, may, might, be possible, be of power.

POWER/GLORY: megaleiotēs *(meg-al-i-ot'-ace)*= *superbness*, that is, *glory* or *splendor:* - magnificence, majesty, mighty power. megaleios *(meg-al-i'-os)*= *magnificent*, that is, (neuter plural as noun) a conspicuous *favor*, or (subjectively) *perfection:* - great things, wonderful works.

The first word for power is Exousia which gives the idea of delegated authority. There is a power that comes from someone saying, "You have the *authority* to carry out what needs to be carried out." The authority flows from the top down. A policeman has authority because our laws have been made and implemented from Washington, the House of Representatives, the Senate, the states and from our Commander In Chief. The same goes for a soldier as he is sent into war, with the authority to defeat the enemy. But if the policeman or the soldier just goes out and attempts to exercise power/authority with nothing to back it up, they will lose. They must have the ability to carry out their authority.

That is where the second word comes in; Dunamis, or dynamic ability. They have the badge or rank insignia that represents the delegated authority, and they have the weaponry/guns to back up the delegated authority with dynamic ability. To be sure, there are those who choose to abuse power, and when they do that, they void the authority that has been delegated to them. The same thing that is true in the world of policemen, is true in the world of karate and the world of Christianity. There are always rogues who deviate from the principles, be they in the dojo, the streets or the Church.

As a Christian, I am called to have both authority and dynamic ability, aka in both cases - power. The disciples received orders from the resurrected Lord and Savior, Jesus the Christ, to go to Jerusalem and wait for power.

"And behold, I am sending forth the promise of My Father upon you; but you are to stay in the city until you are clothed with power from on high."

Luke 24:49

They were obedient and were told of the Exousia and Dunamis.

"He said to them, 'It is not for you to know times or seasons (when he was restoring the kingdom), which the Father has fixed by His own power/exousia/delegated authority; but you shall receive power/dunamis/dynamic ability when the Holy Spirit has come upon you; and you shall be my witnesses both in Jerusalem, and in all Judea and Samaria, and even to the uttermost/remotest part of the earth.

Acts 1:8

"And Jesus came up and spoke to them, saying, All power/authority/exousia delegated authority has been given to Me in heaven and on earth. Go therefore and make disciples of all the nations, baptizing them in the name of the Father and the Son and the Holy Spirit, teaching them to observe all that I commanded you; and lo, I am with you always, even unto the end of the age."

Matthew 28:18-20

Here we see Jesus receiving authority/power from the Father, and He then passes it down to the disciples, who then went to Jerusalem and received the power to do what He told them to do.

The Gospel of Luke shows the contrast of delegated authority (from God) and dynamic ability (of the enemy).

"Behold, I (Jesus) have given you authority/exousia/delegated authority to tread upon serpents and scorpions, and over all the power/dunamis/dynamic ability of the enemy and nothing shall injure you."

Luke 10:19

The title of this chapter is *More Power to Ya*. That is the title of an album and song by the Christian rock group, PETRA. The word, petra, means 'massive rock,' as compared to the name Peter, or petros, which means 'small stone.' Jesus was contrasting the revelation that He was the Christ the living Son of God to Peter who made that confession. Jesus is the massive rock, while Peter was the little stone, and the church would be built on the massive rock of revelation versus the little stone of a human being. (See Matthew 16:13-18) PETRA, the rock group, took on the name as they forged new territory with Christian rock 'n' roll. I will close out this chapter with the lyrics to the song "More Power To Ya," keeping in mind that in karate or in your life, power is needed to accomplish the tasks at hand. Check out the album "More Power To Ya" for the full song.

But good things come to them that wait, Not to those who hesitate, So hurry up and wait upon the Lord/ More power to ya When you're standing on His word, When you're trusting with your whole heart in the message you have heard/ More power to ya When we're all in one accord, They that wait upon the Lord, they shall renew, they shall renew their strength

Words and music by
Bob Hartman, based on Isaiah 40:31

CHAPTER JU ICHI GO (Fifteen)
THE ATTITUDE OF GRATITUDE

Whenever there is an examination at our dojo, the procedure is for the kids to:

(1) run through the examination doing the various katas and techniques
(2) pass the examination
(3) take off their old belts
(4) have their new belts tied on by the Black Belts
(5) Sensai Taylor goes down the line shaking their hands as they look him in the eyes.

Then he talks to them about The Attitude of Gratitude. He reminds them that they need to be thankful for their parents, and all they do and sacrifice for them to bring them to karate. The kids are then sent off to find their parents, give them their old belts, hug and kiss them and thank them.

I like what is being taught at Bill Taylor's Bushido School of Karate. From the moment we walk on the dojo floor as we bow with REI-spect, and as we continue to open and close class with a series of bows, we are saying, *thank you*. We are thanking Master Otsuka for developing Wado Ryu. We are thanking our country for allowing us an opportunity to practice this art. We are thanking Japan, where our art originated. We are thanking our instructors for teaching us. Finally, we are thanking each other for working out together and helping each other train. This Attitude of Gratitude flows from the top; from Mr. Taylor (7th degree), down to the white belts.

I would like to take this time to say thank you to all my instructors and fellow karatekas for being with me on this journey.

ATTITUDE: **1.** manner, disposition, feeling, position, etc., with regard to a person or thing; tendency or orientation, especially of the mind: a negative attitude; group attitudes. **2.** position or posture of the body appropriate to or expressive of an action, emotion, etc.: a threatening attitude; a relaxed attitude.

GRATITUDE: (1) the quality or feeling of being grateful or thankful: He expressed his gratitude to everyone on the staff. (2) Synonyms: thanks, thankfulness, appreciation, gratefulness.

An attitude is something that is developed. It is influenced by people and the environment that we live in as we absorb and adopt an attitude. While we are growing up, our parents are our main sphere of influence, but as we get older, everything from television, movies, video games and our peers begin to shape and develop our attitudes. That's one thing I like about Bill Taylor's Bushido School of Karate. We become a positive influence on the attitude of young people, and sometimes of us old people as well.

Occasionally (but not often, thank goodness), parents come in with bad attitudes that you can see was transferred to their kids. Then those parents wonder why their kids are they way they are and why they act the way they do. Sometimes people (myself included) need an attitude adjustment.

The opposite of an Attitude of Gratitude would be an Attitude of ungratefulness, of being unthankful with no appreciation. This is where the attitude adjustment needs to be targeted. The Attitude of Ingratitude is focused inward, while the Attitude of Gratitude is focused outwardly.

In Philippians 2:3-4 we see how the attitude *should* be.

Do nothing from selfishness/contentiousness.
Do nothing from empty conceit.
Have humility (humbleness) of mind.
Let each of you regard one another as more important than himself.
Do not merely look out for your own personal interests.
Look out also for the interests of others.

This is the spirit (attitude) of Wado Ryu, the Way of Peace and Harmony. It is not self-centered; it is other centered. If only we could have an example of this attitude. Oh, wait; we do have an example - in Jesus. Perhaps better said, if only I would emulate this example more than I do.

Some would say, "Yes, but He is Jesus and I am not." That argument does not hold water. Philippians 2:5 we are commanded to *"Have this attitude in yourselves/among yourselves, which was also in Christ Jesus."* Hmmmm. It seems like a choice that we can have. Let's look at this example of the attitude that we should have, according to Philippians 2:5-6.

He existed in the form of God.
He did not regard equality with God a thing to be grasped.
He emptied Himself.
He took the form of a bond-servant
He was made in the likeness of men/mankind.
He humbled Himself by becoming obedient.
This obedience was to the point of death.
He died on the cross for you.

Of course, this passage is talking about Jesus (God in the flesh) who became a man, became the substitution on the cross in our place for our sins, died, was buried and rose again from the dead. He lowered and humbled Himself to our level, for us. Thankfully, we are *not* called to physically die on the cross. That has already been done. But we become humble when we don't grasp our attitude about who we think we are. We die to ourselves and live for others. The Attitude of Gratitude cannot be lived out as long as we think we are better than someone else. I am not talking about having an appropriate self-esteem. Remember Jesus's words about how we are to love our neighbors (others) *as we love ourselves*. A good Attitude of Gratitude is having confidence in who you are so you can serve others, be thankful to others and to help others.

We take one day each year, as a nation, and celebrate this thing called being thankful. We've turned it into a national holiday, and called it Thanksgiving Day - the day of giving thanks. While having an annual reminder is a good thing, we have plenty to be thankful for on a daily basis. The Attitude of Gratitude should permeate every second, minute, hour, day, month and year of our lives. If we would rise up each day and begin to list all that we are thankful for, then walk in an attitude of thankfulness, what a better place this world would be.

I am thankful for a dojo where I can learn lessons on gratitude. I am thankful that I can express my thankfulness to others instead of passing around negative thoughts and negative actions. I am thankful that I have human examples, and for the example of my Lord and Savior to emulate on planet earth.

CHAPTER JU ICHI ROKU (SIXTEEN)
I'VE GOT DEM NO GOOD, LOW DOWN, MAWASHI GERI BLUES

Back in 1973, I encountered a little trouble (of my own making) that propelled me into taking karate at what was then known as Bushido School of Karate on vine Street in Murfreesboro, Tennessee. I was 22 years old at the time; young, thin, in reasonable health and flexible. There was an emphasis on flexibility and stretching back in the day. We sat on the floor each class and warmed up by having someone stand behind us and push us forward as our legs were stretched out in front of us. We grabbed our toes and leaned to the left, then to the right and finally to the center. We pulled our legs back and laid backwards as we stretched our legs. Then we placed our backs against the wall and put one foot on our partner's shoulder as they slowly rose up, pushing our legs higher. We finished off by putting our shoulders to the wall and pushing our legs up at that angle.

The cause and effect of all of that stretching was flexibility, higher kicks and a more effective Mawashi Geri (round house kick). My dojo at my house was in my basement. I even hooked up a pulley with a rope so I could stretch at home.

Fast forward to 2001. I had turned 50, and was not nearly as flexible as when I was 23 years old. Oh, I stretched, but not as intensely as I did back in the day. The cause and effect was less flexibility. I am now surrounded by younger people in my class. Some are teenagers, others are in their 20s and some are even more mature people in their 30s, while I am now in my 60s. Sometimes it is frustrating and embarrassing when I kick side by side with them and their kicks are more powerful and higher than my kicks. They are kicking to the head and I am kicking to the ankles. If a leprechaun attacks me in a dark alley, I may be able to get in a head shot - if I'm lucky.

This is my excuse for not being able to throw better Mai Geri (front kicks), Yoko Geri (side kicks), Kakato Geri (hook kick/heel kick), Mikazuki Geri (crescent kick), and the dreaded Mawashi Geri (roundhouse kick) - I do *not* consistently stretch, while others do.

I have a friend whom I admire. His name is Joey. Joey is my age, over the years I have watched him improve his kicks. I have watched him make a decision to stretch more, with the resulting cause and effect of more flexible and powerful kicks.

Now I have said all of this to introduce a song that I wrote a few years ago. I sang this song our karate school picnic in the persona of an old blues singer by the name of Blind Lemon Pledge. The folks at the picnic enjoyed it, and I thought you might get a (roundhouse) kick out of it, too.

The song is called:

"I Got Dem No Good, Low Down, Mawashi Geri Blues"

and it goes something like this,

I got dem Mawashi Geri Blues drivin' me out of my mind
I got dem Mawashi Geri Blues drivin' me out of my mind
You say that's O.K. but I know you're just being kind
Well I kick and I kick but my hips don't wanna turn
Well I kick and I kick but my hips don't wanna turn
When I go to class my stomach is like a butter churn

Well I turn my left foot, and I start to kick
The hip won't turn, it feels like a stick
I try to think of excuses, here's the best one yet
I got an old war wound from a rusty bayonet
I said pleeeeze don't make me do it today
I promise to run kata at home
Don't make me Mawashi today I pray
Well you say right foot back, here we go again
Well you say right foot back, here we go again
Mawashi Geri to the head, Hajimai begin
I'm gonna have to play the blues now
(Harmonica)
My toes can't even curl back is it any wonder I'm blue
Mr. Taylor just shakes his head, Mike Wilson does too
Mr. Holt looks in wonder, Karen Wilson is in awe
Mr. Coleman says I object, that kicks against the law
I said pleeeeze don't make me kick it again
I got dem Mawashi Geri Blues
I can't even Ki-Yi on ten

CHAPTER JU ICHI SICHI (SEVENTEEN)
COOKIE DACHI
The Art of Throwing Someone Under The Bus

Wado Ryu karate has roots in Jujitsu. Jujitsu is defined as a method developed in Japan of defending oneself without the use of weapons by using the strength and weight of an adversary to disable him. The origin of the word dates back to 1875, from Japanese jujutsu - ju "softness, gentleness" (from Chinese jou "soft, gentle") + jutsu "art, science" (from Chinese shu "shut"). Some say that a kata like Pinan Yondan was the first kata to introduce Jujitsu concepts. Others argue that First Basic Kata has moves that lean towards the art of throwing.

I remember a movie about an all-girls baseball team back in pre-1950s. In one scene one of the girls started crying, which prompted their coach to yell, "There's no crying in baseball!" After our last examination at the dojo, we take pictures of the students with their new belts. Someone said, "Everybody smile!" We, of course, responded jokingly with, "There's no smiling in karate!" We were playfully referencing the common notion that practitioners of karate are cold, uncaring killing machines with no sense of humor. Perhaps there are some who approach karate that way, but in my experience in the dojo there is lots of smiling in karate, along with laughter, kidding, joking and in general - fun!

Of course, fun must be balanced with hard work, but there is definitely a time and a place for it. I have laughed more than once in a class, and outside of the class, with my fellow karatekas. Humor is a great tool to use to teach the art. In 1973, at the school on Vine Street, that Sensei Newton Harris (who had a great sense of humor), would begin to count in Japanese, imitating Walter Brennan (Grandpappy Amos McCoy on the T.V. show, "The Real McCoys"). When we laughed, he made us stop and do push-ups.

One of the running gags at our school is called, Throwing Someone Under the Bus, and we call the stance to do the throwing, Cookie Dachi (a variation on a move in Chinto). The origin of this Bus Throwing started innocently enough, then escalated to monumental proportions. During one of our examinations at the school, I mentioned Mr. Paul O'Gratton (International Man of Mystery) that Sensei Herzer had not instructed the students run the Kiso Kumite Kata (a kata run with a partner that has torre (attack) and uke (defense). For some inexplicable reason, Mr. O'Gratton felt compelled to reveal in public to Sensei Herzer, that '*Rodney said you forgot to run Kiso Kumite!*' To which Sensei Herzer responded, as he turned and looked at me, 'Oh, did he?'

Bam! I was officially thrown Under The Bus, and Mr. O'Gratton has forever become known as the *Father Of the Bus Throw.*

Note: Mr. O'Gratton, aka Paul Gratton, is a good friend and brother in the Lord, with a delightful English accent.

On another occasion Mr. O'Gratton threw me under the bus with Sensei Taylor. You must understand that our honor and love for Sensei Taylor is mixed with a healthy dose of fear and awe. You can run every kata perfectly, but as soon as Sensei Taylor puts his eyes on you, you will make every mistake and error possible. On this occasion, Mr. O'Gratton graciously presented me with a copy of Sensei Taylor's new book, "Wado Ryu: A Fighter's Perspective," and even had it autographed for me. The inscription read, *To Rodney, Thank you for all your support over the years. Your friend, Bill Taylor.*

As we sat in the outer room of the dojo, I flipped through the book, looking at the pictures. I jokingly said to Mr. O'Gratton, "I believe that Mr. Taylor's stance is wrong in this picture." Of course, the stance was spot-on perfect, so the irony of the statement was funny. Sensei Taylor walked by at that moment, and I thanked him for his book and the autograph. All was well until, Mr. O'Gratton said, *'Mr. Boyd pointed out that your stance was wrong.'* Mr. Taylor's response was, 'Oh, did he?'

Bam! Thrown under the bus again.

Another friend at the school is Mr. Joey "Big Foot" Mount of the Lion (Monteleone). Joey is my age, and is someone I want in a foxhole with me. He is loyal and funny. Years ago, while I was sparring Joey, he took his big foot and kicked me in the chest. The story (and I'm sticking to it) is: after the chest-kicking incident, I went home and I took off my shirt. "What happened to you? Exclaimed my lovely wife, Brenda. I looked in the mirror, and saw a red impression of Mr. Monteleone's footprint on my chest. Every chance I get, I tell the story and throw Joey under the bus. I have retold this story so many times that it has grown to epic Bus Throw proportions. But don't feel sorry for Mr. Monteleone. He has a black belt in bus throwing.

JOKE BREAK

Mr. Monteleone: I skipped four grades in school.
Me: Really?
Mr. Monteleone: Yeah. Some of you call it, college.

I always laugh, no matter how many times I have heard this one. And who says there is no smiling, laughing or fun in karate?

Somewhere along the way, the stance used to throw someone under the bus was named Cookie Dachi. The stance was adopted from Kokutso Dachi (back stance), with the arms drawing back and slicing sideways and forward - as you throw someone under the bus. The cookie concept comes from someone mentioning that Sensei Coleman loved a certain type of cookie. The next session with him someone brought those cookies, and someone *else* actually took credit for baking them.

Mr. O'Gratton had some cookies that he showed us, and he informed us that he was going to present them to Mr. Coleman before the class officially got under way. He had them safely tucked away in his bag, to be brought out at the most opportune time. I stole the cookies from his bag and hid them in my uniform as we lined up. As Mr. O'Gratton feverishly looked for the cookies, I stepped up and I said to Mr. Coleman, "I know how much you enjoy these cookies and I would like to present them to you." I drew out the stolen cookies, looked back to Mr. O'Gratton, and flashed a little knowing smile.

Bam! Under the bus once again as Mr. Coleman thanked me over and over.

Bacon is also a theme that has been repeated at the dojo many times. While not officially and Under the Bus move, it still brings a smile to our lips. Mr. Brian "Bacon Boy" Williams is the focus of this food fun.

Brian loves bacon, so anytime we can work bacon into the conversation concerning him, we'll do it. When Mr. Williams was testing for his most recent belt, I walked over to his wife and friends and mentioned that Brian would be awarded his Bacon Belt today. Little did I know that one of his friends was a photographer, and that a picture would soon appear on Facebook - of Brian with a belt made out of bacon wrapped around his waist.

The Bible speaks of this thing called laughter, a merry heart, and their effect on our bodies and our life in general.

"A happy heart is a good medicine and a cheerful mind works healing, but a broken spirit dries the bones."

Pro-Verbs 17:22 (AB)

"A glad heart makes a cheerful countenance, but by sorrow of heart the spirit is broken."

Pro-Verbs 15:13 (AB)

"All the days of the desponding afflicted are made evil (by anxious thoughts and foreboding), but he how has a glad heart has a continual feast (regardless of circumstances)."

Pro-Verbs 15:15 (AB)

CHAPTER JU ICHI HACHI (EIGHTEEN)
THE VALUE OF VIRTUES

One thing (among many) about our school that I love is that we do not just teach karate. The physical kicks, punches, blocks and self-defense is only one aspect. As we have seen previously, the intention of the student is more than just learning karate. It is about developing virtues, as outlined in another section within our student guide entitled "Black Belt Virtues." Virtues are defined in Dictionary.com as:

(1) moral excellence; goodness; righteousness.
(2) conformity of one's life and conduct to moral and ethical principles; uprightness; rectitude.
(3) chastity; virginity: *to lose one's virtue.*
(4) a particular moral excellence. Compare cardinal virtues, natural virtue, theological virtue.
(5) a good or admirable quality or property: the virtue of knowing one's weaknesses.
(6) effective force; power or potency: *a charm with the virtue of removing warts.*
(7) virtues, an order of angels.
(8) manly excellence; valor.

The martial artist, the student of karate, makes declarations beyond the physical.

"As a dedicated student of the martial arts, I will live by the principles of black belt." (Black Belt Virtues)

Notice that the declaration is a specific *choice* to live a *lifestyle* with the guiding light of *principles*. There are six principles that we will now check out.

MODESTY

This thing called *modesty* is a call to decency. A modest person is not prone to vanity or being boastful. There is a lack of being arrogant when you are

> "As a dedicated student of the martial arts, I will live by the principles of black belt."
>
> (Black Belt Virtues)

modest. The way we usually think of being modest is in the way we dress, but it also refers to the concept of decency in behavior, the way we act. Sometimes when you begin to learn karate there is the opportunity to think that you are a "bad ass." Some get cocky and arrogant, but the heart of karate, and what we are taught, is to become humble versus haughty.

The Bible underscores the lessons I have and continue to learn in the dojo.

"At that time the disciples came to Jesus, saying, 'Who then is greatest in the kingdom of heaven?' And He called a child to Himself and stood him in their midst, and said, 'Truly I say to you, unless you are converted and become like children, you shall not enter the kingdom of heaven. Whoever then humbles himself as this child, he is the greatest in the kingdom.'"

Matthew 18:1-4

"But the greatest among you shall be your servant. And whoever exalts himself shall be humbled, and whoever humbles himself shall be exalted."

Matthew 23:12

"But He gives a greater grace. Therefore it says, God is opposed to the proud, but gives grace to the humble."

James 4:6

"Humble yourself in the presence of the Lord, and He will exalt you."
James 4:10

"Humble yourselves, therefore, under the mighty hand of God, that He may exalt you at the proper time."
I Peter 5:6

Modesty, humbleness, is the key to people who will be lifted up and recognized for their character - whether it be as a student of karate or a disciple of Christ.

COURTESY

Courtesy is the way you act towards someone, the way you behave yourself, the way that you show respect to another person. Courtesy is your character manifested to others. Of course, courtesy can be faked, much like Eddie Haskell on the old T.V. show "Leave it to Beaver." Eddie would always be courteous to Wally and the Beaver's mom and dad, but once they leave his true character comes out.

Remember this - character is *not* how you act in front of others as much as it is how you act when you are alone.

Behavior is the way you conduct yourself. Mom use to tell me to, "Behave yourself." In the dojo, we show courtesy and REI-spect to one another. That is one thing that I see many young people learning at the dojo - a development of character, respect and courtesy for themselves, their parents, their peers and people in general. It doesn't come naturally to human beings. It is a process that must be reinforced before it becomes second nature. If there is no discipline at home, or if for whatever reason a student does not act like they should, they receive structured, consistent reminders about being courteous to one another. The belts of higher ranks are examples of being courtesy by doing something as simple as saying 'Yes sir,' instead of 'Uh-huh." Many parents can testify to the change in their child's behavior at home after studying karate.

The Apostle Paul wrote a letter to his son in the faith, Timothy, giving him some fatherly guidance on how to act. He told him first to discipline himself for the purpose of godliness.

This self-discipline means to "practice naked," like the athletes in the Greek games who would disrobe so they would not get tripped up or entangled by their flowing clothes. Paul later when on to encourage Timothy to,

"Let no one look down on your youthfulness, but rather in:
(1) speech
(2) conduct
(3) love
(4) faith
(5) purity
show yourself an example of those who believe.

I Timothy 4:12

In the light of this thing called courtesy, we see that how we conduct (behavior) ourselves and what we allow in our lives that would taint our purity is rooted in common courtesy.

INTEGRITY

Integrity is something within you that guides you to act a certain way, based on principles of morals. Your integrity is based on your belief system and manifested in your character. If you compromise your code, it could be said that the integrity of your character has been compromised. Integrity is doing the right thing based on your guideline/code that is within you. This thing called integrity is woven into the lessons our instructor's teach us. We sometimes play a game with the kids call Senpai Says (kind of like Simon Says). If the youngster misses a move they are asked to do, he or she must sit down. They must also sit down if they do something when Senpai did *not* Say. Sometimes the child will miss the move, will *not* sit down. The instructor will turn that into a lesson about integrity, even if they were not seen. It is pretty amazing to watch the kids begin to learn the lesson.

Biblical integrity is important for our preservation, our unwavering walk, to be in His presence, for guidance in our walk.

INTEGRITY: tôm *(tome)= completeness;* figuratively *prosperity;* usually (morally) *innocence:* - full, integrity, perfect (-ion), simplicity, upright (-ly, -ness), at a venture.

"Let integrity and uprightness preserve me, for I wait for Thee."
Psalm 25:21 *(KJV)*

"Vindicate me, O Lord, for I have walked in my integrity; and I have trusted in the Lord without wavering."
Psalm 26:1

"As for me, Thou dost uphold me in my integrity, and Thou dost set me in Thy presence forever."
Psalm 41:13 *(KJV)*

"So he shepherded them according to the integrity of his heart and guided them with his skillful hand."
Psalm 78:72

"The integrity of the upright will guide them, but the falseness of the treacherous will destroy them."
Pro-Verbs 11:3

"A righteous man who walks in integrity, how blessed are his sons after him."
Pro-Verbs 20:7

SELF-CONTROL

Self-Control is defined as. "control or restraint of oneself or one's actions or feelings." The only one who can control you - is you. Oh, someone can dominate you, maybe even force you to do something, but that is not self-control. It is other-control. The idea of control is "to exercise restraint or direction over, to dominate, command. To hold in check; curb (i.e. to control a horse; to control one's emotions)."

If you are not under self-control, then you are out of control. When I go up and down the floor throwing techniques or doing kata, I begin to breathe heavier as I try to suck more oxygen into my lungs. It seems like the harder that I try to breathe, the more out of breath I become. I huff and puff and gasp for the next breath. That's when I hear a little voice in my head, that sounds like Senpai Mike Wilson, reminding me to, "Control your breathing. Don't let your breathing control you."

Sometimes during a sparring session, a student will go after his partner like they are in a street brawl. It's a bad idea; much better to fight with control and focus. You can spar with passion and still be in control. Trust me, you don't want one of our instructors to control you. You would much rather implement self-control - self-restraint.

In the Manufacturer's Handbook (aka The Bible) we see that one of the fruits (results) of the Spirit is self-control or temperance.

SELF-CONTROL: Egkrateia *(eng-krat'-i-ah)= self control* (especially *continence*): - temperance. egkrates *(eng-krat-ace')=strong in* a thing *(masterful)*, that is, (figuratively and reflexively) *self controlled* (in appetite, etc.): - temperate.

There is a verse in the book of Pro-Verbs (Positive-Action) that speaks of restraint - self-control. It says, *"Without a vision the people perish, but happy is he who keeps the law."*

The word perish means to be unrestrained, so it reads, "Without a vision the people are unrestrained (or out of control), but happy is he who keeps the law."

We have a saying in the Ruminator Sunday School Class, "Unrestrained thoughts (what we think) produce unrestrained words (what we say), resulting in unrestrained actions (what we do)."

Thoughts, words, and actions, when out of control produces trouble. Self-control takes control of what goes into our minds, takes control of what we say and takes control of what we do. Flip Wilson, the comedian, made famous the saying, "The devil made me do it." What he was saying was that it is not my fault. Someone else (the devil) was controlling me.

In the dojo, the lesson is clear, we need to control the way we act within the dojo, the way that we act with one another and the way that we act outside of the dojo. We need to begin to practice self-control.

PERSEVERANCE

To complete my journey for the coveted prized of the black belt, perseverance was a key virtue that I needed, because many times - and even sometimes now - I wanted to give up. If it was not for my instructors and my fellow karatekas, I would have quit and gone back to just dreaming about a black belt versus actually having attained the prize around my waist.

PERSEVERANCE: proskarterēsis *(pros-kar-ter'-ay-sis)*= *persistency:* - perseverance. proskartereō *(pros-kar-ter-eh'-o)*= to *be earnest towards,* that is, (to a thing) to *persevere, be constantly* diligent, or (in a place) to *attend* assiduously all the exercises, or (to a person) to *adhere* closely *to* (as a servitor): - attend (give self) continually (upon), continue (in, instant in, with), wait on (continually).

Perseverance is what we need from the very first time we attempt to run the First Basic Kata. As we learn how to turn to the left with a low block, how to move forward with a moving forward front punch, how we turn around in the other direction with a low block without falling down and running through the entire 20 moves in the kata - we need perseverance. Why? Because if you don't get passed the First Basic Kata you will never progress to the next level, and the next level, all the away to the black belt.

Perseverance is merely *keeping on keeping on* in the face of obstacles and hardships. Perseverance is the act of *giving up on giving up.*

The Apostle Paul, wrote about continuing on in the face of sufferings.

"I press on toward the goal for the prize of the upward call of God in Christ Jesus."

Philippians 3:14

INDOMITABLE SPIRIT

The indomitable spirit goes hand in hand with perseverance. Really, if you think about it, all of the virtues interweave with each

> The belt is an outward representation of the inward reality.

other, like many cords that twine together to produce one strong rope. Indomitable is an adjective that means, "that which cannot be subdued or overcome, as persons, will, or courage; unconquerable: an indomitable warrior." (Dictionary.com) Spirit is defined as, "an attitude or principle that inspires, animates, or pervades thought, feeling, or action: the spirit of reform." (Dictionary.com)

We are taught techniques that will help to defend us in the heat of an attack. We practice these things over and over again, until hopefully they become second nature. I asked Mr. Wilson many years ago, if he had ever had to use his martial arts training and if so what was it like? His response to me, "It was messy." You have the have a mind-set of victory. Not in the sense of a cocky, arrogant, *I'm better than you.* But you do need to have an attitude that nothing will subdue you, that nothing will overcome you, that no person or thing will defeat you. I have heard that if you enter the ring to fight an opponent, if you don't have this indomitable spirit, you have already lost the battle.

Concerning my faith, which overflows in all that I am and all of my activities in life, I am more than a conqueror.

"Who shall separate us from the love of Christ? Shall tribulation, or distress, or persecution, or famine, or nakedness, or peril or sword? Just as it written, For Thy sake we are being put to death all day long; we were considered as sheep to be slaughter. But in all these things we overwhelmingly conquer/ more than conquer through Him who loved us. For I am convinced that neither death, nor life, nor angels, nor principalities, nor things present, nor things to come, nor powers, nor height, nor depth, nor any other created thing, shall be able to separate us for the love of God, which is in Christ Jesus our Lord."

Romans 8:35-39

MORE THAN CONQUERORS: hupernikaō (*hoop-er-nik-ah'-o*)= to vanquish *beyond*, that is, gain a decisive victory: - more than conquer.

There are many things trying to conquer you. The threat is real and the potential to give up is real. What turns us from being defeated to victor is an indomitable spirit.

The indomitable spirit has what is known as a 'can do' attitude. I have heard more than once, 'Can't do - never did anything.'

"I have strength for all things in Christ Who empowers me - I am ready for anything and equal to anything through Him, Who infuses inner strength into me. [that is self sufficient in Christ's sufficiency."

Philippians 4:13 (*AB*)

The Black Belt Virtues are:
(1) modesty
(2) courtesy
(3) integrity
(4) self-control
(5) perseverance
(6) indomitable spirit.

They are good attributes for us to reach for, grasp and practice. In the New Testament there is another list of attributes that underscores and solidifies the Black Belt Virtues. In the book of Galatians there is a list of what is known as The Deeds of the Flesh that we are encourage *not* to practice. They include:
(1) immorality/sexual immorality
(2) impurity
(3) sensuality
(4) idolatry
(5) sorcery
(6) enmities
(7) strife
(8) jealousy
(9) outbursts of anger

(10) disputes
(11) dissensions
(12) factions/heresies
(13) envyings
(14) drunkenness
(15) carousings

Galatians 5:19-21

Those are the kinds of things that can bring a virtuous man down. That's why we need to have the contrasting fruit of the Spirit front and center in our lives. The Black Belt Virtues in the Student Handbook begins with a pledge and declaration that, "As a dedicated student of the martial arts, I will *live* by the principles of Black Belt..." then it lists the six virtues. I have found in my own personal life, that I can't live without the help of the Holy Spirit, the Comforter, the *paracletos* - the One called along side to help.

COMFORTER: parakletos *(par-ak'-lay-tos)*=An *intercessor, consoler:* - advocate, comforter

The Holy Spirit (Big S) who dwells within our human spirit (little s) is our intercessor, our consoler, our advocate, our comforter. Our relationship with the Holy Spirit bears fruit (outworking of the relationship him with Him).

"But (in contrast to the deeds of the flesh) of the Spirit (Big S) is (1) love (2) joy (3) peace (4) patience (5) kindness (6) goodness (7) faithfulness (8) gentleness (9) self-control - against such things there is no law."

Galatians 5:22-23

Here are some quick definitions from Strong's Concordance of each one.

LOVE: agapē *(ag-ah'-pay)*= *love*, that is, *affection* or *benevolence*; specifically (plural) a *love feast:* - (feast of) charity ([-ably]), dear, love. agapao *(ag-ap-ah'-o=)*Perhaps from ἀγαν agan (*much*; or compare to *love* (in a social or moral sense): - (be-) love (-ed).

JOY: Chara *(khar-ah')= cheerfulness*, that is, calm *delight:* - gladness, X greatly, (X be exceeding) joy (-ful, -fully, -fulness, -ous). chairo *(khah'ee-ro)* A primary verb; to be full of *"cheer"*, that is, calmly *happy* or well off; impersonal especially as a salutation (on meeting or parting), *be well:* - farewell, be glad, God speed, greeting, hail, joy (-fully), rejoice.

PEACE: eirēnē *(i-rah'-nay)*=Probably from a primary verb εἴρω eiro (to *join*); *peace* (literally or figuratively); by implication *prosperity:* - one, peace, quietness, rest, + set at one again.

PATIENCE/LONGSUFFERING: Makrothumia *(mak-roth-oo-mee'-ah)= longanimity*, that is, (objectively) *forbearance* or (subjectively) *fortitude:* - longsuffering, patience.

KINDNESS: chrēstotēs *(khray-stot'-ace)= usefulness*, that is, moral *excellence* (in character or demeanor): - gentleness, good (-ness), kindness.

GOODNESS: agathosune *(ag-ath-o-soo'-nay)= goodness*, that is, *virtue* or *beneficence:* - goodness. agathos *(ag-ath-os')*=A primary word; "good" (in any sense, often as noun): - benefit, good (-s, things), well.

FAITHFULNESS: Pistis *(pis'-tis)= persuasion*, that is, *credence*; moral *conviction* (of *religious* truth, or the truthfulness of God or a religious teacher), especially *reliance* upon Christ for salvation; abstractly *constancy* in such profession; by extension the system of religious (Gospel) *truth* itself: - assurance, belief, believe, faith, fidelity. peitho *(pi'-tho)*=A primary verb; to *convince* (by argument, true or false); by analogy to *pacify* or *conciliate* (by other fair means); reflexively or passively to *assent* (to evidence or authority), to *rely* (by inward certainty): - agree, assure, believe, have confidence, be (wax) content, make friend, obey, persuade, trust, yield.

GENTLENESS: praotēs *(prah-ot'-ace)= gentleness*; by implication *humility:* - meekness. Praos *(prah'-os)=gentle*, that is, *humble:* - meek.

SELF-CONTROL/TEMPERANCE: Egkrateia *(eng-krat'-i-ah)=*From *self control* (especially *continence*): - temperance. egkratēs *(eng-krat-ace')= strong in* a thing *(masterful)*, that is, (figuratively and reflexively) *self controlled* (in appetite, etc.): - temperate.

There you have it; six Belt Virtues and nine Fruits of the Spirit. Each one is a work in us that manifests itself in every area of our lives. Of all the Virtues and Fruits listed there is one that stands out, and if you walk in that one Virtue/Fruit all of the others will fall into place. Which one do you think it could be? Well, let me end the suspense. It is *love.*

THE LOVE CONNECTION OF A VIRTUOUS MAN/WOMAN

"But now abide faith, hope, love, these three; but the greatest of these is love."

I Corinthians 13:13

LOVE: agapē *(ag-ah'-pay)= love*, that is, *affection* or *benevolence*; specifically (plural) a *love feast:* - (feast of) charity ([-ably]), dear, love. agapao *(ag-ap-ah'-o=)*Perhaps from ἀγαν agan *(much*; or compare to *love* (in a social or moral sense): - (be-) love (-ed).

You may be asking yourself - *Self; what has love got to do with karate and martial arts?* Well, I'm glad that you asked. One of the lessons I have learned as I have watched Mr. Taylor and other instructors over the years, is their motivation. Oh, to be sure, the motivations are multi-faceted, but I have seen one motive called love. I have heard it mentioned more than once from more than one instructor. Love for the kids, love for their art, love for the camaraderie - love on many different levels is prevalent to me. That's how it is in real life also. You must have love as the primary motivator or you will be consumed by hate. In the absence of love is *fear*.

"And we have come to know and have believed the love which God has for us. God is love, and the one who abides in love, abides in God, and God abides in him. By this, love is perfected with us, that we may have confidence in the day of judgment; because as He is, so also are we in this world. There is no fear in love, but perfect love casts out fear, because fear involves punishment, and the one who fears is not perfected in love. We love - because He first loved us."

1st Epistle of John 4:16-19

LOVE DEFINED (I Corinthians 13:4-8)

The love mentioned many times in the Bible as God's love for us is called "agape" - the unselfish, giving love.

"For God so loved the world that He gave His only begotten Son, that whosoever believes in Him should not perish, but have everlasting life."

John 3:16

Here is the portrait of the characteristics - the virtues - of love that should be our guideposts:

Love is:
(1) patient
(2) kind
(3) not jealous
(4) does not brag
(5) not arrogant
(6) does not act unbecomingly
(7) does not seek it's own (way)
(8) is not provoked
(9) does not take into account a wrong suffered
(10) does not rejoice in unrighteousness

(11) rejoices with the truth
(12) bears all things
(13) believes all things
(14) hopes all things
(15) endures all things
(16) *Love never fails.*

CHAPTER JU ICHI KU (CHAPTER 19)
THE ART OF SELF DEFENSE

Back in 1972, the catalyst that compelled me to take karate was a physical attack upon my person. I was 21 years old at that time, and trying to find out who I was and what I wanted to be when I grew up. A couple of years before I had come to the end of my rope emotionally, and needed a change. I had mixed emotions about life. I had been raised in the church. At one point my parents attended church and took me. They eventually stopped going, but I did not. I enjoyed the peaceful atmosphere of the church, while my home life was chaotic. Adults at church were friendly and offered me structure and direction. There was music, Sunday school, friends from school, so church was not just a spiritual endeavor, but a social event for me.

When I was 16, I decided to quit going to church. After all, my parents didn't go, and my perception of churchgoers (including adults and my peers) had changed. I now viewed them all as a bunch of hypocrites. One thing led to another, one bad choice resulted in another bad choice, one abandoned virtue made it easier to jettison another virtue. Each step led me inexorably down the path of non-Christian activity - aka *sin*.

Then I met Brenda. We dated, started going steady and I wanted to get a little closer to her so I started going to church with her. One thing led to another and I "got saved." I went away to Bible school - then I dropped out of Bible school.

Oh, I still loved the Lord, but as I chased one religious experience to another I got burned out. In religious terminology I was a *backslider*. In secular terminology I took face forward dive into the pool of sin. I smoked more dope, drank more booze, sniffed more chemicals and paint thinners, and did more stupid stuff under the influence than I ever did before I became a Christian.

Which leads us to the catalyst for me taking the martial arts.

I received a call (as a result of a stupid act while under the influence) at 2:00 in the morning from a man who wanted me to meet him somewhere so he could, "beat my ass." I politely declined. He informed me that he would get me at work. I hanged up the phone while shaking in my boots (actually I was not in my boots, but in my bare feet, but you get my meaning).

My lovely bride (we had just got married in August of 1972) wanted to know who was on the phone. To be honest, I can't remember what I told her, but I did not get much sleep for the rest of the night. I got up, went to work and walked around the factory all day long looking over my shoulder in fear of the potential attack.

The attack didn't come, and I was somewhat relieved when 3:00 rolled around and the workday was over. I clocked out, walked out, climbed into my faithful, green Chevrolet Vega, started it up and drove out the gate. There, across the street, waiting for me, was my worst nightmare - the guy who had called and the woman who started all of my problems (actually, it was me that started my problems - they just wanted to end them, by ending me). I turned right onto the road, drove to the main intersection, then turned left. The guy followed close behind me, trying to force me over.

I thought perhaps if I pulled over I could reason with him and end the problem. *Wrong!* He got out of his car and approach me. I rolled down my window to *talk* with him, but before I got out the first word, his fist was in my mouth.

Since the rolling down the window to reason with him had worked *so* well, I decided to open my door and get out of the car so I could reason with him. That's when I discovered a valuable, eternal truth - you cannot reason with anger.

This guy was over six foot tall and towered over me like Goliath over David. He looked every bit the image conjured up by the term, "redneck." To add insult to injury, he had brought a friend with him. I was taller than his little partner, but two-against-one are never great odds, and to be honest, even at one-against-one odds were still against me.

The tall one began intimidating me with his words, saying that he was going to teach me a lesson and beat my boo-tay (he didn't actually use the term, *boo-tay*, and in all fairness, he never once touched my butt). Fists began to fly and I tried to block them. I knew nothing, no thing, zilch, nada, zero about self-defense. I was merely trying for self preservation.

Remember that this was at quitting time, and there were lots of other companies letting out at the time, so the roads were congested with people getting off work. And all of them had a ringside seat to watch this Main Title Event which was taking place in front of God and everybody. I caught a glimpse of the factory that I had just left, and all of my co-workers were lined up to watch.

In desperation I took a wild, roundhouse swing (doing my best to make a fight out of it), and I connected! Unfortunately, my little finger has been crooked from birth, and I did not have it tucked in as tight as it should have been. I caught the tip of my little finger on the big guy's chin, and knocked it completely out of joint. It crooked out to the left. I took one look at my finger and actually said to him, "You messed up my finger."

"I'm gonna mess up more than your finger, boy," he replied, and the the fight continued.

I blocked using the *Rod Uke* method of blocking - that is, doing anything that worked. I managed to get in another punch that connected on his chin and mouth area. The big guy fell. It felt like everything kicked into slow motion, almost like Goliath being hit between the eyes with a smooth stone from David's sling. As he fell, a loud cheer erupted from my fellow co-workers who were watching the fight.

I turned, expecting the big guy's little friend to attack me, but he put up his hands and said, "I'm not gonna mess with you."

I turned back around to see the big guy wiping blood from the corner of his mouth as he got back to his feet.

"You done messed up, boy," he said. (He did not say actually say "messed up." He was using "F" word in all it's glory).

But instead of renewing the fight, the big guy just turned and walked toward his car. His his girlfriend stuck her head out of the window and shouted a warning.

"Run! He's coming for his gun."

Gun? Yikes. Double yikes!

I hopped into my faithful green Vega, turned the key - and it would not turn over. I felt like Marty McFly trying to start his time machine car in "Back to the Future." I tried a couple of more times and it finally started. I speed away (as much as you can speed away in a Vega), and I looked in my rear view mirror and I saw this tall, angry, redneck chasing me on foot with a tire iron, swinging it and cussing at me. It would have been laughable, except for the fact that I was scared to death.

I was so embarrassed by this event that I never went back to my job. I think Brenda went and got my last pay check. I went into hiding after that, partially out of shame and embarrassment, but mostly out of - fear.

They say that time heals all wounds, and that might be at least partially true. Time passed and my physical wounds healed, but while the fear and shame eased up some, they were ever-present inside me. I had experienced first-hand the theoretical premise of what is known as *cause and effect* or *sowing and reaping*. I *knew* not to do the things that I did that brought me to the point of being the Main Event on the side of the road, but I made a choice. I chose to drink. I chose to get drunk. I chose to do things that I should not have done. I fully acknowledge that what happened on the side of the road that day - I deserved. It was a wake up call to my dormant spiritual nature. What happened next was a merger of a return to my spiritual life and my entrance into a life-long dream of pursuing the martial arts.

My spiritual return was based on prayers of a friend, Gary Montgomery, and a bunch of his friends (who did not know me from Adam), interceding for my return. Gary was a Christian who worked at the factory. He had watched me fall. He saw me on a picket line at the factory, with a picket sign in one hand and a beer covered by a paperback in the other. I once gave Gary all of my Bible study books and told him I was leaving the faith. To make a long story short (too late), I later repented of my sins, received forgiveness and called Gary to ask if he still had my books.

"I've got them waiting for you," he said.

To this day, Gary and Rena are still good friends and we attend the same church.

Around the time of my humiliation, I read a small advertisement in the Daily News Journal about karate lessons at a place called Bushido School of Karate. The course cost $15.00 a month, and I needed some self defense. The instructor, Newton Harris, was a guy I new from school and the neighborhood.

When I started on my dream and desire to learn self defense, it was purely so I could learn to defend myself. It was completely motivated by fear and a desire for vengeance. This book, "Never Run a Dead Kata," and all of the lessons I learned in the dojo, show the fundamental shift in my motives. Years ago, I wrote a paper called "Spiritual Self Defense (SSD)." If I had only had the SSD in action earlier in my life, I may have avoided a number of painful lessons. On the other hand, I might have never done the thing that, by the grace of God, brought me down the path to where I am this day.

SPIRITUAL SELF DEFENSE

We are under a spiritual attack from the enemy. According to John 10:10 the thief comes to steal, kill and destroy. According to Ephesians 6:11,12 there are strategies/deceits and schemes of the devil (little d) against us. According to Ephesians 6:12 we are not wrestling with flesh and blood, but contending against the despotisms, powers, master spirits and spirit forces of wickedness in the heavenly, supernatural sphere. We are told in Ephesians 6:13 that we are to put on armor, to resist, to stand our ground and to stand firmly in place. According to I Peter 5:8 there is a devil (little d) roaming around like a lion, roaring (intimidating) and seeking someone to seize upon and devour. We are told not to passively sit by and be devoured, but to withstand him, to be firm in faith against his onset, rooted, established, strong, immovable and determined.

In the natural we have weaponry. In karate (empty hand) we have nine physical weapons:
(1) head
(2) right hand
(3) left hand
(4) right elbow
(5) left elbow
(6) right knee
(7) left knee
(8) right foot
(9) left foot

In the spirit we have a series of nine weapons that work in conjunction with each other:

Gifts of the Spirit (I Corinthians 12:1-10)

Word of Wisdom
Word of Knowledge
Faith
Gifts of Healings
Effecting of Miracles
Prophecy
Distinguishing of spirits
Tongues
Interpretation of tongues

Fruit of the Spirit (Galatians 5:22,23)

Love
Joy
Peace
Patience
Kindness

Goodness
Faithfulness
Gentleness
Self Control

THE POWER SOURCE

We have power to accomplish our self defense. There are two words that apply to our power source:

Exousia: delegated authority
Dunamis: Dynamic ability

Exousia gives us the right to exercise our dynamic ability. In the physical realm it is like a police officer who that wears a symbol of that delegated authority - his badge. That badge represents the legal authority or right to do his job. Dunamis is the weaponry, the fire power, that he has the right to utilize to defend himself and us from the enemy.

Just because we have the physical and spiritual right to defend against the enemy does not mean that the enemy readily submits to us. There may be a fight involved and we must be trained, ready and willing to walk in obedience.

FINAL THOUGHTS ON SELF DEFENSE

DEFENSE: Apologia *(ap-ol-og-ee'-ah)*= a *plea* ("apology"): - answer (for self), clearing of self, defense.

"And who is there to harm you if you prove zealous for that is good? But even if you should suffer for the sake of righteousness, you are blessed. And do not fear their intimidation and do not be troubled, but sanctify Christ as Lord in your hearts, always being ready to make a defense to everyone who asks you to give an account for the hope that is in you, yet with gentleness and reverence."

I Peter 3:14-15

Wado Ryu (the way of harmony and peace) is being ready to bring peace in the safest, least restrictive manner that we can. It is discipline of the whole man, to flow in the river of peace, by avoidance rather than direct conflict.

CHAPTER JU KU KU (TWENTY)
THE END IS THE BEGINNING

Most movies and stories conclude by saying The End. Well, here we are with Chapter 20, the final chapter. We are coming to The End of our book. In 1972 I started at Bushido School of Karate for my introduction into the world and study of the Way of Peace and Harmony called Wado Ryu. After a brief hiatus - of around 39 years - I re-entered my study at Bill Taylor's Bushido School of Karate. From 11/15/2001 to 10/29/07 I studied, practiced, laughed, cried, moaned and groaned as I learned my lessons in the dojo.

I walked into the Broad Street dojo, or rather I limped in (remember my knees had been under attack), with my bag and signed in for the examination. I entered the locker room - the same one where I started many years ago - and changed into my uniform, much like a matador or gladiator in preparation for the big fight. A thousand thoughts flooded my mind, as a million butterflies fluttered in my stomach, churning up nervous energy waiting to be channeled into this one moment.

I slowly wrapped my brown belt around my waist and made my way out to the warm-up floor of the dojo. This was the room where my many teachers took an older, overweight, slightly nervous man, and began to mold him into a martial artist. I began to stretch out and run kata and techniques while talking with some of the other examinees. I saw various fellow students who had come to support me and to offer words of encouragement. I can't tell you how much that meant to me. At one point, I looked over at the door and I saw a man with a completely bald head smiling at me. It took a few seconds before I realized, that it was Sensei Newton Harris, my first instructor from the old Vine Street School. I walked over, shook his hand, hugged him and asked him, "What are you doing here?"

"I heard you were testing today," he responded. "I would not have missed it for the world."

Wow, I really had come full circle on my journey, the journey that I had begun in 1972 and was now ending in 2007.

I stepped onto the main dojo floor where there were many people ready to take the test. I looked out into the outer area through the wrap-around glass windows, and the place was packed with people there to cheer on their loved ones. My wife Brenda, my son Phillip, my pastor Bruce Coble, and a large number of my fellow karatekas and instructors were there. It was then that I confessed to Mr. Taylor that my knee was injured.

"Don't let them see you limping!" he encouraged me intently.

The command to line up was given, and we all took our positions. Among the seven Black Belts who stood before us, I only recognized two familiar faces; Sensei Herzer and Sensei Taylor. I kept hearing the words of Sensei Coleman's "Don't be intimidated by anybody, including anyone in the examination with a black belt around their waist." Over and over Mr. Coleman had told me that we knew the material, we were ready for the examination and that we would pass, so don't let someone try to intimidate you. He also told me that if I made a mistake, don't stop. Keep going, act as if you ran your kata perfectly. Another word of advice was that if someone asked you to run your kata over, .don't let that rattle and shake you. It could be you made a mistake, or it could be that they have *never* seen that kata ran as good as you ran it. I actually did leave out some moves in a kata (although I can't remember which one), and I acted like I owned that kata. I was blessed that I did not have to run it over.

The Sunday after I took my federation examination, I walked out of the dojo on Broad Street still wearing a Brown Belt. On Monday, we were told to come back and then we would know for certain whether we had passed the examination. In the back of my mind I *thought* that I had passed, but I just was not 100% sure. I could not imagine being told to come there on Monday, only to have the rug pulled out from underneath me by not being awarding the coveted prized.

The house was packed with Black Belts and there was electricity in the air. I put on my uniform and wrapped around my waist my brown belt with the five tips of electrical tape symbolizing that I was ready to test. We were called forward to stand before the examiner, they explained the procedures, and then we bowed and the exam began. It was all a blur, but I took Mr. Taylor's advice and to not limp (it must have been the adrenaline kicking in) and to have spirit. If *spirit* was translated as *sweat*, I had a whole lot of *spirit*.

I had a friend take pictures during the examination (which is a major no-no) and the look of intensity on my face said it all. I remembered that I did not look much at the examiners, but instead maintained the *thousand-foot stare*. For a little encouragement, I looked over at Sensei Herzer and Sensei Taylor. I also glanced over at Melanie Lepp, who was from the school and was taking the examination with me. You can really draw strength from familiar faces.

Once the examination was over we bowed out and met with Mr. Taylor. We were instructed to come back the next night.

We were not told whether or not we passed, and we certainly did not ask. Many pictures were taken that day, with Brenda and Phillip, with Sensei Harris, with Mr. Wilson and Mr. Maxwell, with Sensei Taylor and of course the group shot with all the brown belts who took the examination with me. We looked tired, exhausted, sweaty and relieved.

The next night I came into the school, the same way I had the previous day. I went into the locker room, put on my uniform and tied on my brown belt for the last time - I hoped. I stepped to the main dojo floor, which was packed with Black Belts from both schools. We were called forward and told to take off our old belts, fold them and put them around our necks. We had been through 10 or more previous examinations and had done this same ritual before. At that point Sensei Taylor and others, wrapped the coveted prize, the black belt that I had in my mind for years, around my waist. The emotions were overwhelming.

Sensei Taylor congratulated us. Then he dropped the bomb on us.

"Now, you are ready to learn."

This was not The End of our journey. It was just the beginning. All of the blood, sweat and tears from November 15, 2001 to October 29, 2007 had merely prepared us for The End - of the Beginning.

Each of us newly minted Black Belts were paired with a seasoned Black Belt, and we began to learn our new kata - Chinto. I limped through that new kata. My left knee was hurting, my shoulders were aching, but inside the spirit of Bushido was flowing. I was pumped!

I eventually ended up going to an orthopedic physician, had MRI on my knee, took shots in my shoulders and had surgery on my left knee. I had everything from torn ACL, torn meniscus, arthritis and general floating crude in my knee. After surgery, and appropriate period of time for healing, I came back to class to continue my journey. I was raring to go, and attacked my first class back with such intensity that I pulled my hamstring. Ouch! I persevered and by April 16, 2011 I received my 2nd degree (Ni Dan) Black Belt.

During all that time, one thing had remained constant: the lessons were still being taught and the lessons were still being learned in the dojo. The interesting thing that I am still learning is that the old lessons that you learned long ago - still apply.

That's the way it has been since I became a Christian in 1970. There were good times, there were bad times and there were ugly times as I walked out my faith. Lessons were learned, and are still being learned, along the way. More than 40 years later I am still standing, still believing. The End of my life as a non-Christian was just the Beginning of my life as a believer. The old things in my life passed away, and new things came and are still coming.

"Therefore, if any man/wo-man/hu-man is in Christ they are new creations. The old things passed away. Behold. New things have come (and are constantly coming)."

II Corinthians 5:17

"The Lord's loving kindnesses indeed never cease, for His compassions never fail. They are new every morning; Great is thy faithfulness."

Lamentations 3:23

"Therefore we do not lose heart, but though our outer man is decaying, yet our inner man is being renewed day by day."

II Corinthians 4:16

I have found that God is the God of eternity - the God of eternal life.

ETERNITY: 'ad (*ad=*) properly a (peremptory) *terminus*, that is, (by implication) *duration*, in the sense of *perpetuity* (substantially as a noun, either with or without a preposition): - eternity, ever (-lasting, -more), old, perpetually, + world without end.

"He has made everything beautiful/appropriate in its time. He has also set eternity in their heart, yet so that man will not find out the work which God has done from the beginning even to the end."

Ecclesiastes 3:11

EVERLASTING/ETERNAL: = aiōnios (*ahee-o'-nee-os*) *perpetual* (also used of past time, or past and future as well): - eternal, for ever, everlasting, world (began).

"For God so loved the world, that He gave His only begotten Son, that whosoever believes in Him should not perish but have everlasting life."

John 3:16

On the time-space continuum, way back in 1970, I stepped into the timeline of eternity; a timeline that had been going way before I ever stepped into it. When I became born again (saved, redeemed, etc.) I entered into a new realm. My old life, from 1951 to 1970 was The End of the Beginning. I started elementary in 1957 and finished high school 1970. I was not the best of students, but I did pass and did graduate. I eventually went on to finish Graduate School and earn my Masters of Education (how ironic).

When my wife, Brenda, introduced me to the Lord by leading me down the "Roman Road To Salvation" (Romans 3:10, Romans 3:23; Romans 5:12; Romans 6:23; Romans 10:6-17), I left my old life and entered my new life. I was at last ready to learn, and I have been learning lessons in the dojo of my life ever since; even to this day. I currently have the honor to teach white belts on Friday and Saturdays. I am blessed to be part of the testing process of those on various legs of their journeys to The End of their Beginning.

After receiving my Ni Dan rank (2nd degree Black Belt) I am more challenged than ever. It seems like everything that could stand in my way has happened. My physicality, my work schedule, my emotional state of being and a plethora of other obstacles have appeared as roadblocks to my forward advance toward the next level.

The next degree that I am pressing towards is the 3rd degree Black Belt. It took me four years to go from Sho Dan to Ni Dan. If my track record holds true, and if I get on the horse and ride and do what I need to do, I will be 65 years old before I reach that next level. How can I possibly accomplish this? One thing is sure, I will have to take the previous lessons that I learned in the dojo, and continue to learn new lesson. I'll have to persevere. And

> "I believe God made me for a purpose, but he also made me fast. And when I run, I feel His pleasure."
>
> - Eric Liddle

never give up. And walk in the spirit shout mindset. And stand in the indomitable spirit.

I will prevail, but. I can't just *think* about it, *wish* for it to happen, *pray* about it and *expect* it to happen. I must set my faith into actions, step back out onto the dojo floor and *do* it!

I would like to end "Never Run a Dead Kata (Lessons I Learned in the Dojo)" with the last paragraph from my black belt topic - "What Earning a Black Belt Means to Me." My hope is that as you read this book, it will be a source of encouragement, and that it instills hope for you to live your life out loud with the faith and tenacity to never give up and always keep learning.

My real purpose and power, comes from my faith and love for God (Father, Son, Holy Ghost). Eric Liddle, a runner in the 1924 Olympics in Paris and later to be a missionary to China, whose life was chronicled in the movie "Chariots of Fire," is a source of inspiration for me. He stated, "I believe God made me for a purpose, but he also made me fast. And when I run, I feel His pleasure."

I am not fast, but I do feel His pleasure when I work out and compete. Liddle also offered the secret of his success, and I hope it will also be the secret to my success.

"The secret of my success over the 400 meters is that I ran the first 200 as hard as I could, and then the second 200 (with God's help) I ran it harder."

RESOURCES AND REFERENCES

I would like to take this time to list resources and references that I have used and learned throughout the years. A lot of it was just the daily practice of what I learned in the dojo, but much is from various books, people, websites and experiences.

Sensei Bill Taylor's book "Wado Ryu: A Fighter's Perspective" - This book is a history lesson for karate and specifically Wado Ryu karate, a story of one man's journey, and a technical manual for the principles behind the techniques. I have been blessed to be able to hear many of these lessons from the mouth of the man himself in class.

Bill Taylor's Bushido School of Karate website at www.bskonline.com

Two books by Mr. Shingo Ohgami (recommended by Mr. Taylor in his book). Mr Ohgami was instructed by Master Hirinori Otsuka. Both of these books were invaluable on my journey. They are (1) "Karate Katas of Wado Ryu" (2) "Introduction to Karate"

The book by Master Hironori Otsuka who originated our style of karate, Wado Ryu. The book is called "Wado Ryu Karate." The first part of the book is the philosophy of this art followed by a primer on stances, hand techniques, leg techniques, and then the meat of Wado, the kata. I will always be grateful for his wisdom when he stated, "Never run a dead kata."

Sensei Cecil T. Patterson, who was commissioned by Master Otsuka to establish the United States Eastern Wado-Kai Federation in 1968, was responsible to Master Otsuka for the operation and teaching in all Wado kojos of the Eastern United States. In 1974 Mr. Patterson wrote a book called "An Introduction to Wado-Ryu Karate." It is a practical manual for the basics, plus insight into the Ippon and Kiso Kumite Kata and a step-by-step overview of Pinan Nidan.

The website for United States Eastern Wado-Kai Federation, currently under the leadership of Sensei Cecil T. Patterson's son, Sensei John Patterson (assumed upon the death of his father) is www.useasternwado.com

The Manufacturer's Handbook - aka The Bible - aka The Word of Father God. As I learned my lessons in the dojo, I learned at the feet of the true Master, Lord and Savior - Jesus Christ.

All of the instructor who have ever taught me have been valuable resources to me. They were, and still are, always there and ready to answer any question that I ever had. They literally had to have the patient of Job as I fumbled my way down the road to the black belt.

To my band of brothers and sisters, who when they have learned things at a quicker pace than me, always helped me when I asked them to show me what I was doing wrong. Even to this day, as I am attempting to learn Passai and Wanshu, they always take time to help me.

Various dictionaries, lexicons, concordances, including "Vine's Expository Dictionary of New Testament Words" (Published without copyright in 1940) and "Strong's Exhaustive Concordance of the Bible" (public domain) - as a Speech-Language Pathologist words mean a lot to me.

And last, but not least, one of the greatest resources that I have is the ultimate Teacher - the person of the Holy Spirit.

"And as for you, the anointing which you received from Him abides in you, and you have no need for any one to teach you; but as His anointing teaches you about all things, and is true and is not a lie, and just as it has taught you, abide in Him."

I John 1:27

I'm convinced that the *Teacher*, the *Anointing*, is the Holy Spirit who dwells within me, and *All Things* includes anything I have and will learn inside the dojo, inside the church and out in the world.

Wow. I cannot believe that this is the end of the book. One last shout-out. One of my pastors at Springhouse Worship and Arts Center, Ms. Barbie Loflin, is responsible for taking my hand and guiding me thorough the process of fulfilling this dream. Without her, this would just be another writing that would not see the light of day. I want to thank Mike and Paula Parker of WordCrafts Publishing for putting flesh on the skeleton of my dream. Without them I would still be handing out spiral bound copies to whoever would take one.

Check out these inspirational titles from WordCrafts Press
(www.wordcrafts.net)

Why I Failed in the Music Business
(and how NOT to follow in my footsteps)
By Steve Grossman

Youth Ministry is Easy!
(and 9 other lies)
By Aaron Shaver

Chronicles of a Believer
By Don McCain

Illuminations
By Paula K. Parker & Tracy Sugg

Made in the USA
Charleston, SC
24 June 2014